3234543

THE BRUTE
and
Other Farces

By Anton Chekhov

EDITED BY ERIC BEN~

in ne~
Eric Bentley a

SAMUEL FRENCH, INC.
45 WEST 25TH STREET   NEW YORK 10010
7623 SUNSET BOULEVARD HOLLYWOOD 90046
LONDON   TORONTO

CONTENTS

APOLOGIA

1.

EXCEPT for some later revisions in the dialogue, Chekhov's seven one-act farces belong to the years 1886–1891, which immediately precede the 'major phase' when the famous full-length plays were written. Like the funny stories which he signed 'Chekhonte' because he was a little self-conscious about them, these little plays are admittedly 'minor Chekhov,' though one makes the admission with a sinking heart in an age which makes a cult of the 'major'— the notion of the major, anyway—in order to excuse its lazy reluctance to read any man's collected works. One would not deny that 'The Best Plays of Chekhov' contains just what it says it does, but one might assert that a reader should no more be content to sit down with that book than a parent should be content to sit down to dinner with only his best children.

It is never wise for an author to give a modest account of himself: the critics accept it. The lighthearted Chekhonte was discounted long ago. Anton Chekhov is played on Broadway and in the West End in a vein of soulful somnolence. The adjective 'Chekhovian' can convey any shade of mournful emotionality from the wistful to the lugubrious; it never suggests the sunny, the zany, the skittish, the wildly destructive, though Chekhov in fact was famous for these qualities even before the others showed themselves.

In a recent collection designed to modify and correct the prevailing view of Chekhov, Mr. Edmund Wilson finds 'his true weight and point' in his last, most sombre, and most sociological works. It is high time, I conclude, to protest against the tendency of modern critics to overlook the obvious. Mr. Wilson did exactly the same thing in his study of Dickens years ago. His new Dickens was to interest us as a man involved in psychoneurotic conflict.

And today there is a fairly widespread assumption that a writer of funny stories—or melodramatic ones—is scarcely worth a critic's attention. Farce and melodrama have come to be valued, if at all, as embellishments of more earnest and more tortured books. One critic makes a favourite of *Hard Times*, ostensibly because of its superior (that is, more Jamesian) structure. One cannot resist the conclusion, however, that he prefers dark moods to more frivolous ones as more becoming to the serious business of Literature, not to mention Criticism. This is to be seduced by *l'esprit sérieux*. *The Pickwick Papers* may be incommensurable with *Hard Times*, but surely is no more inferior to it than *Don Quixote* is inferior to *Madame Bovary*?

Even in the most serious works of Chekhov, as of Dickens, farce and melodrama are not embellishments added later to a structure of more 'literal' substance. One might plausibly maintain, on the contrary, that the structure itself is farcical and melodramatic and that it is the seriousness which is superadded. But at this point the notion of addition is itself misleading, for, in a fully realized masterpiece, nothing is merely stuck on; all is, finally, of a piece. At any rate, once we see that the role of farce in certain non-farcical masterpieces—from Molière and Dickens to Shaw and Chekhov—is a large and reputable one, we are free at last to view farce in its pure state as a large and reputable phenomenon.

2.

Not that its state often *is* pure. Labiche has kept French schoolteachers busy for a long time now distinguishing between his 'true farces' and his 'comedies of character'. The poor man himself seems to have been terribly confused on the point. And Chekhov takes no greater pains to stay within boundaries staked out by pedagogues. In the latest of the plays printed, here, *The Celebration* he is taking his leave of farce forever and launching out, as we sense in reading it, towards his masterworks. He made six versions of *The Harmfulness of Tobacco*, the earliest of our plays, each one more serious than the last*. Even *The Brute* and *Marriage Proposal* are a mass of psychological details such as no average farceur would use.

How far Chekhov's individuality carried him from the regular article can be demonstrated by comparing *The Brute* with its 'source'. The play was suggested to Chekhov by a performance of a French one-act farce: *Les Jurons de Cadillac* by Pierre Berton (1865). Here the principal joke is that the man—already a suitor for the lady's hand at the outset—can't refrain from swearing for more than a few seconds at a time. The action of the play consists of the lady's offering to marry him if only he can hold himself in for one hour. The climactic twist in the action comes when the man fails to meet the demand in such an amiable way that the lady is charmed by him, and the curtain comes down as she herself swears one of his great oaths. The jest seems almost simpleminded compared with Chekhov's. And to tell a less simple story, Chekhov has recast the dramatic action entirely, and placed it in a different, more actual social setting. He has, as we say, 'made more of it', and that 'more' includes a good deal that, by any standard, is serious.

Yet, if it is possible to overlook the serious elements in a Chekhov farce, it is also possible to be obsessed with them. Actors are sometimes tempted to play *Swan Song* or *The Harmfulness of Tobacco* as wholly pathetic outpourings. The wrongness of the interpretation is proved by the fact they find themselves forced into making cuts. When the lecturer in *Tobacco* is exclusively pathetic, the actor has to omit 'business' that is inevitably grotesque, such as his stamping on his jacket and showing the audience the rents in the back of his waistcoat. To be consistent he should also omit parts

*It is the final version that is printed here. Avrahm Yarmolinsky has printed the first in *The Unknown Chekhov* (New York, 1954).

of the text too, for only the license of farce permits—for example—the number thirteen to recur so madly.

In some ways, *Swan Song* is an even subtler case. Here the pathos is more unabashed. Yet a touch of the utterly ridiculous is necessary not merely to the texture but to the characterization. Those who think that farce always coarsens and simplifies should note that it is farce, in this play, that makes the characterization complex.

Chekhov's skill in the mixing of the elements is nowhere more remarkably apparent than in his *re*-mixing of them when he makes over one of his own stories into a play. Perhaps the most interesting instance is *Summer in the Country*, which was made out of a story called *One of Many*.* Mr. Magarshack interprets the changes as an attempt to 'preserve the decencies of the stage', for, in the story, Tolkachov's load includes a child's coffin, and the poor fellow grumbles that he will probably never get paid for it. But there are reasons for omitting this which go far beyond the matter of moral propriety. A child's coffin on stage, Chekhov must rightly have felt, would carry a higher charge of painful emotion than a farce can stand. Chekhov also knew his stagecraft, and might have concluded that no actor could manage a coffin in addition to half a dozen other impedimenta.

On one point, however, I agree with the Magarshack interpretation. In the story, as a climax to her various persecutions, the wife presents her lawful claim to Tolkachov's person at four in the morning. Chekhov's omission of this poignant incident in the play can surely be taken as a concession to the squeamishness of nineteenth-century audiences. I have smuggled it into the script printed here. And I will report an experience that would have no public importance except that it shows rather vividly how Chekhovian work

Swan Song and *The Celebration* are also adaptations of Chekhov stories—*Kalkhas* and *A Helpless Creature*, respectively. In *The Wedding* he draws on two stories (*A Marriage of Convenience* and *A Wedding with a General*) and a sketch (*The Marriage Season*). For further particulars, see David Magarshack's two books on Chekhov: *Chekhov the Dramatist* and *Chekhov: a Life*.

depends upon a balance that is very easily upset: re-instating this single 'point', I was tempted to put back other things as well, but I soon found myself in danger of destroying the farcical tone of the play without substituting any other.

Chekhov's whole life in the theatre might be seen, not as an exercise in tragi-comedy as traditionally conceived, but as a search for a kind of drama in which tragic and comic elements lose their separate identities in a new, if nameless, unity. Even a title may vibrate with the energy of this search. The play now under discussion is called in the Russian original: *The Tragedian in Spite of Himself*, on the pattern of *Le médecin malgré lui*. Farce is here the form imposed on a potentially tragic situation. But only potentially tragic. The play does not resemble one of Eugène Ionesco's tragic farces in which the despair is deeper than the humour or the love. It is not a tragedy 'in spite of' the farcical form, for Tolkachov is not a tragic figure but a tragedian, a play actor, one who sees himself as tragic, a victim of self-dramatization and self-pity, a comic figure. (With all this in mind, I very much wanted to keep the original title. But, since there has never been a plausible translation of Molière's title, it seemed foolish to follow one of the implausible ones in translating Chekhov. My title is derived from Chekhov's subtitle, and my subtitle is more or less a quotation from Tolkachov, the play being, in reality, not a tragedy but a farce.)

In fine, Chekhov's farces, if they are minor, cannot, as such, be dismissed. His greatest plays have a farcical component, and his slightest farces have something in them of the seriousness, pathos, and even subtlety of the greatest plays. In some ways simple, they are not one-sided but dialectical. The critic who judges them and the director who stages them must have a dialectical mind in order to grasp the constant conflict and synthesis of elements. In its fine balance of contrasts—particularly of the pathetic and the ridiculous—a Chekhov farce might be regarded as a full-fledged Chekhov drama in miniature.

3.

This book, it should be conceded at once, is not a contribution to scholarship. My collaborator knows no Russian at all and, though I myself can struggle through a Russian text with the aid of a dictionary, I am, by the same token, quite insensitive to many nuances both of meaning and feeling. If the propriety of our having made this collection were questioned, however, we should defend ourselves somewhat as follows.

We are not people who believe that 'anything goes'. For example, we believe that it would have been improper for us, in our ignorance, to have tampered with the more refined sort of literary masterpiece. We do not have designs on Lermontov and Pushkin. Farces, we thought, were in a somewhat different category. And, for that matter, scholarly translations of Chekhov's farces already exist for those who wish to consult them. We are not even Constance Garnett haters. I consider Mrs. Garnett generally under-rated; but she did have a fatal defect in the particular department of farce. She had no sense of humour, or none that affected her renderings of comic language. Some of the funniest things in literature would never, in her versions, raise even a crooked smile.

Impressed with certain qualities in a play of Theodore Hoffman's called *Rich But Happy*, I told him I thought he should go to work on some of Chekhov's little comedies. One day, not long afterwards, the mail brought me the text of *Marriage Proposal* which is now printed in this book. I found it funny, and it was the first time I had found any of Chekhov's farces funny. I had seen that they had stories, plots, characterizations that *might* have exploded in laughter, but I had also noted wearily that the explosions never occurred. I now saw why: these fireworks had been placed in the damp cellar of uncomic language. A certain style of vocabulary and, even more, a certain rhythm of phrases and speeches has to be established by the dialogue before the larger jokes of situation and character can take effect. Without a word of Russian, Mr. Hoffman had found a vocabulary and the rhythm that 'worked.' In common with more qualified judges, I tend to think that he had intuitively discovered what was in the Russian original, but, even if this is not so, and even if scholars are right when they shout (as they will) that the Russian is quite different, I still think that I was justified in wanting to publish the Hoffman text. I would not deny that so-called faithful versions have a certain reference-value for students even when, in their fidelity, they betray their author's very spirit. I ask the scholars to grant the value of 'unfaithful' versions as defined here. To the objection that it would be possible perfectly to combine scholarship and comedy in this field, I would retort: prove it. Up to now it has certainly not been done. Our final word on our efforts is: *faciant meliora potentes*.

E.B.

The Harmfulness of Tobacco

A LECTURE
(1886–1902)

ENGLISH VERSION
by ERIC BENTLEY

The Harmfulness
of Tobacco

*The lecturer has long side whiskers but no moustache. He
wears an old threadbare frock-coat. He makes a majestic
entrance, bows to his audience, adjusts his waistcoat.*

Ladies and, so to speak, gentlemen, the suggestion was made
to my wife that I should give a popular lecture here for
charity. Well, why not? If I must lecture, I must, that's all.
It's all one to me. I'm not a college professor, it's true. I
can't say I have a university degree, but, nevertheless, I've
worked on scientific problems for thirty years, much to the
detriment of my health, I might add. Thirty years work on
strictly scientific problems! I'm very fond of abstract
reasoning. From time to time, I even write scientific articles,
well, not strictly scientific, but, if you'll pardon the expression, approximately scientific. Incidentally, I wrote quite a
long article only the other day. It's called: The Harmfulness
of Certain Insects. My daughters like it a lot, especially the
part about bedbugs. But I just read it through and tore it
up. What's the use? What difference does it make whether
such things are written or not? You still have to use insect
powder. We have bedbugs even in the grand piano . . .

As the subject of my lecture this evening, I have chosen:
The Harmfulness of Tobacco. The damage done by tobacco
to the human race. I'm a smoker myself, but my wife told
me to give a lecture on the harmfulness of tobacco, so there's
nothing else for it. If I must lecture on tobacco, I must,
that's all. It's all one to me. As for you, ladies and, um,
gentlemen, I want to appeal to you to take my lecture very,
very seriously. If you don't, pretty terrible things can happen

3

to me. But if anyone here present doesn't like the thought of a dry, scientific lecture, he may put on his hat and go home.

[*Adjusts his waistcoat*]

Is there a doctor present? If there is, I want him to pay particular attention: I may be able to teach him something. Tobacco, in addition to being very harmful, is used in medicine. For example: place a fly in a snuff-box, and what happens? It drops dead. Why? Well, I suppose it has a nervous breakdown . . .

Tobacco, speaking very generally, is a plant . . .

Yes, I know, when lecturing before an audience, I blink a little bit, my right eye blinks. Pay no attention, it's just nervousness. I'm a nervous man, speaking very generally. This blinking began in 1889. On the 13th of September, to be absolutely exact. The day my wife presented me with our fourth daughter, Barbara. All our daughters were born on the 13th . . .

However,

[*Looking at his watch*]

the time at my disposal this evening is strictly limited and I mustn't stray from the subject of the lecture . . .

I think I should tell you that my wife runs a music school and also a private boarding school, well, not a boarding school precisely, it's really a . . . well, it *is* a kind of boarding school. Between you and me, my wife likes to tell people how hard up she is, but she's put something away for a rainy day, I'd say forty or fifty thousand, oh yes. As for myself, I haven't a ruble, I haven't a kopeck. But why talk about that? My sphere of influence, so to speak, is the housekeeping. I do the marketing, keep an eye on the servants, write up the accounts, stitch exercise books together, exterminate as many bedbugs as possible, take my wife's lapdog for walks, catch mice . . . One of my little duties last night, for instance, was to issue butter and eggs to the cook for today's dinner. To make pancakes with. Well, to cut a long story short, when the pancakes were ready—today, that is—

my wife comes to the kitchen and says three of the girls can't have pancakes because they have swollen glands. So it looks as if we have quite a few pancakes too many! What to do with them? At first, my wife tells me to put them in the pantry. Then she thinks it over a minute, and says to me: 'Oh, eat them, eat them, you dumbbell!' When she's in a bad mood, she calls me dumbbell. Or viper. Or Satan. Now, what sort of a Satan am I? Eh? She's *always* in a bad mood. I didn't eat those pancakes, I swallowed them. I wolfed them down without chewing. I'm always hungry. Yesterday, for example, she gave me no dinner at all. 'A dumbbell like you,' she said, 'doesn't deserve a dinner' . . .

However,

[*Looks at his watch*]

I see I have strayed a little from the subject of the lecture . . . To proceed . . . though I know you'd all rather hear a love song. Wouldn't you? Or some symphony or other? Or an aria?

[*He breaks into song*]

> Hear ye the battle cry?
> Forward! Be strong!

I don't recall where that comes from . . . Incidentally, I forgot to tell you what I do besides the housekeeping. I teach mathematics, physics, chemistry, geography, history, tonic sol fa, literature . . . and so on. My wife charges extra for singing and dancing, though the teacher of singing and dancing is your humble servant. Our address is Five Dogs Lane, Number 13. That's probably the reason I'm a failure—living at Number 13. My daughters were all born on the 13th. I think I told you. Our house has 13 windows . . but why go on?

Appointments with my wife can be set up at any hour. The prospectus can be had for 30 kopecks from the janitor.

[*Takes brochures out of his pocket*]

I can let you have them right now, if you like. 30 kopecks a copy. Who'd like one? Well . . . 20 kopecks.

[*Pause*]

What a shame!

Yes, Number 13. I seem to be no good at anything. And now I've grown old and stupid. Just look at me, giving a lecture, to all appearances very happy and bright, but, inside, I'd like to scream at the top of my voice, I'd like to run away to the ends of the earth! There's no one I can open my heart to. I often feel like crying. What about your daughters, you say? Well, what about them? I tell them all this, and they just laugh! . . . We have seven daughters. Sorry, six. No, it's seven. Anna, the eldest is twenty seven. The youngest is seventeen. Ladies and gentlemen,

[*Looks around*]

I'm unhappy, I've grown to be a fool, a nonentity, but at the same time you see before you the happiest of fathers! That's how it *should* be, and who am I to say it isn't? Oh, if you only knew! My wife and I have been together thirty three years, and I am glad to report they were the best years of my life. Well, not the best, but, speaking very generally . . . They have passed, in a word, like a single happy moment and, strictly speaking, well, curse them, curse them all!

[*Looks around*]

I don't think she's here yet. No, she isn't: I can say what I please! I'm frightened of her. I'm frightened when she looks at me. Well, as I was saying, my daughters are pretty slow about getting themselves married, probably because they're shy and men can't get near them. My wife doesn't like giving parties, she never invites anyone to dinner, she's stingy, ill-natured, shrewish . . . That's why no one ever comes to see us. Let me tell you a secret.

[*Comes down to the footlights*]

Christmas and Easter, you can meet our daughters at their aunt's house. Their aunt's an old lady with rheumatism. She wears a yellow dress with black spots that look like beetles. Covered all over with black beetles.

[*In a whisper*]

Refreshments are served! You can eat! And when my wife isn't on hand, you can . . .

[He raises his fist to his lips]

I get drunk on one glass, and, you know, I feel so wonderful, and at the same time so sad, I can't tell you how sad! I remember my youth for some reason or other. And I feel like running away. If you only knew how I long to run away!

[With enthusiasm]

To run away, throw everything over, and never, never look back! Where to? It doesn't matter! Anywhere! Just to be away from this stupid, petty, wicked MISER, my wife, who's been tormenting me for thirty three years! To get away from the music, the kitchen, and all her money! From this silly, trivial life we lead! And to stop, somewhere far away, in the middle of a field, to stand there under the wide heavens like a tree, a post, a scarecrow, and watch the bright, gentle moon overhead and forget, just forget . . . Wouldn't it be wonderful not to remember *anything*? You know what I'd like to do now? Take my coat off! This miserable old coat that I wore at my wedding thirty three years ago and that I'm still wearing to give lectures in for charity!

[He tears it off]

Take, that, coat!

[He tramples on it]

And that! I am old, poor, pathetic—like this waistcoat that's all shabby and worn behind.

[He turns around to show the back of his waistcoat]

It's not that I want anything. I'm better than this, I'm a superior sort of man, and at one time I was young, intelligent, I went to the university, I had my dreams, I thought of myself as a human being . . . Today, I don't want *anything*, unless it's peace and quiet—peace, quiet, rest.

[He looks around, and quickly puts on his coat]

I'm afraid my wife's in the wings, waiting for me.

[Looks at his watch]

My time's up . . . If she asks you, will you tell her the lecture was . . . will you tell her that her fool of a husband . . . I mean, that I . . . conducted myself with dignity?

[*Looks towards the wings, clears his throat*]
She's looking at me.

[*He raises his voice*]
In view of the fact that, um, tobacco contains the terrible poison which I have just described, it is best to refrain from smoking under any and all circumstances. And I hope I may conclude, so to speak, that my lecture on the Harmfulness of Tobacco will have been of some use to you. That's all. Dixi et animam levavi.*

[*He bows and stalks majestically out*]

---

*' I have spoken and got a load off my mind.' But, since the lecturer would not openly say this in the presence of his wife and the audience, the line must not be delivered in English. A 'Lecturer', Professor Leon Stilman advises me, is probably a graduate of a classical Gymnasium; in which case he would have had eight years of Latin. [E.B.]

Swan Song

A DRAMATIC STUDY
(1887–1888)

ENGLISH VERSION
by *THEODORE HOFFMAN*

CHARACTERS

Vassily Vassilyitch Svetlovidov, *an old actor, 68.*
Nikita Ivanitch, *a prompter. An old man.*

Swan Song

The empty stage of a second-rate provincial theatre, littered with the remains of the evening's scenery and various backstage tools and equipment. There is a stool, upside down, in the centre of the stage. It is night, and dark. Svetlovidov, in the costume of Calchas (the renegade Trojan soothsayer), comes from the wings, holding a lighted candle, and laughing.

SVETLOVIDOV: Well, what do you know about that? What a come-down! Falling asleep in the dressing room! The show's over, the theatre's empty, and there I am, snoring my head off. What a clown! What a clown! Just a dull old dog, that's all. Must have gotten so crocked that I dropped off in my chair. Sheer brilliance, old boy—a natural born genius for amounting to nothing. [*Shouts*] Yegorka! Yegorka! Where are you, you devil? Sleeping it off somewhere, the scoundrel. May all the devils in hell and one old witch burn you alive, you ingrate! Yegorka!

[*Gives up, turns the stool over and sits on it.*

Puts the candle on the floor]

Not a sound. No answer but that confounded echo. And only today I gave him three rubles because he took such good care of me. Tonight you couldn't find him with bloodhounds. I suppose the theatre's locked up, too. The skunks! [*Shakes his head*] Ooof! Drunk! What do you know? Gave me a benefit and I showed my gratitude by pouring a ton of wine and beer down my gullet. Wine and beer, ugh! I'm shaky all over and my mouth feels like there's been an army camping in it. Positively revolting! [*A pause*] Stupid, that's what it is, stupid! The old clown gets tight as a coot and when you ask him ' Why?'

11

he doesn't know. He just did it, as usual. Ooh! God, my
back aches, I've got the shivers, and my heart feels as
damp and dark as a cellar. Well, if you've no regard for
your health, you might take pity on your old age, Pagliacci,
my boy! [*Pause*] Old age . . . You can pretend all right,
put up a big front, clown around for them, but you've
lived your life, old boy. There's no getting around that!
Sixty-eight years shot straight to hell! No double-your-
money-back on that sale! The bottle is empty and there's
just a few old dregs at the bottom. That's the story in a
nutshell. Whether you want the role or not, the only part
they're going to let you rehearse from now on is that of a
corpse. The Grim Reaper is waiting in the wings. [*A
pause. Looks in front of him, out into the auditorium*] You
know, I've been on the stage for forty-five years, and I
do believe this is the first time I've ever been alone in a
theatre in the middle of the night. First time. What do
you know? Pretty spooky! [*Goes up to the footlights*] Can't
see a thing! Well, there's the prompter's coop, . . . I can
see the first box, now . . . and the conductor's podium . . .
everything else is pure darkness. A black, bottomless pit,
like a tomb in which death itself lies hidden . . . Brrr, it's
cold. The draught blows out of there like it does out of a
chimney. What a place for a seance! A haunted house, if
there ever was one! Sends shivers down my spine!
[*Suddenly shouts*] Yegorka! Yegorka! Where the hell are
you, you devil! Good Lord, what am I doing talking about
Hell and the Devil here for? Watch your language! Cut
out the drinking! You're old! It's time to die! People who
are sixty-eight spend their time in church, preparing for
Death! And you? Cursing your head off, face wracked up
with a hangover, dressed up in some Greek clown's outfit.
How's that for a sickening sight? Better get a move on and
get into some decent clothes. Still, it certainly is spooky.
If you were stuck here all night you could die of fright.

[*Starts toward the wings. As he does*, NIKITA IVANITCH

comes on stage in a long white bathrobe. SVETLOVIDOV
utters a cry of terror and staggers back]
Who are you? What do you want? Who are you after?
[*Half angry, half pleading*] Who are you?

NIKITA: It's only me.

SVETLOVIDOV: [*Still terrified*] Who are you?

NIKITA: [*Slowly approaching him*] It's me, the prompter,
Nikita Ivanitch . . . Vassily Vassilyitch, it's me . . .

SVETLOVIDOV: [*Sinks helplessly on to the stool, breathing hard,
trembling all over*] Good God, who is it? Oh, it's you, you,
Nikitushka? What are you doing here?

NIKITA: I sleep in the dressing rooms, but, please, for God's
sake, don't tell the manager. I don't have anywhere else
to stay, so help me God, I don't.

SVETLOVIDOV: So, it's only you, Nikitushka . . . Good God!
Good God! Listen! I got sixteen curtain calls tonight,
three bunches of flowers, and God knows what other junk.
They loved me! And then not one of them went out of
his way to wake up an old drunkard and take him home . . .
I'm old, Nikitushka, old! I'm sixty-eight! Sick as a dog,
and ready to give up the ghost! [*Leans on* NIKITA, *half-
crying*] Don't leave me, Nikitushka. I'm old, and helpless,
ready to die . . . It's dreadful, dreadful . . .

NIKITA: [*With respect and sympathy*] It's about time you
went home, Vassily Vasillyitch.

SVETLOVIDOV: What for? I don't have a home! Hah, a home!

NIKITA: You mean you can't remember where you live?

SVETLOVIDOV: Of course, I can, but who wants to go there?
Not me! Look, Nikitushka, I'm alone in the world. No
family, no wife, no children, no one! I'm alone, like the
wind in the fields. Who's going to pray for me when I
die? No one! And let me tell you something! Being alone
scares me stiff. No one to buck me up, or give me a little
sympathy, or put me to bed when I'm drunk. Who do I
belong to? Who needs me? Who gives a damn about me?
Nobody, that's who, Nikitushka, nobody!

NIKITA: [*Through tears*] The public loves you, Vassily Vassilyitch.

SVETLOVIDOV: The public? The public's at home in bed, asleep. And they're not dreaming about this old clown, either. No, nobody needs me, nobody gives a damn about me. I don't have a wife, and I don't have any children.

NIKITA: Well, why feel so bad about that?

SVETLOVIDOV: Because I'm a man! I'm alive! There's blood in my veins, not water! And good blood, too. I'm a gentleman, Nikitushka. I come from a good family. Before I fell into this black hole I was in the Army, an artillery officer. What a figure I cut then! Young, handsome, courageous, full of spirit! Whatever happened to that young man? And after that, well, I was quite an actor in my day, wasn't I, Nikitushka? Quite an actor! And whatever happened to him? Whatever happened to my life, for that matter? Where's it all gone to? [*Getting up and leaning on* NIKITUSHKA] You know, I looked out there a little while ago and my whole life was spread out before me. This confounded black hole has swallowed up forty-five years of my life, Nikitushka! And what a life! I can look out into that darkness there and see every detail of it, clear as I see your face. For example: Youth! Ideals, faith, strength, cockiness, and women! And what women, Nikitushka!

NIKITA: Isn't it time you went to sleep, Vassily Vassilyitch?

SVETLOVIDOV: When I was a young actor, bursting with enthusiasm, a woman fell in love with me for my acting alone. Would you believe it? A society girl: elegant, slim as a birch tree, young, innocent, all that, but as full of fire as a sunset in summer. Nikitushka, there was a creature! Eyes such a delicate blue that if you thought of them on a dark night it seemed daylight. An exquisite smile, and wavy hair. Let me tell you about that hair. You think the waves of the ocean are powerful? Well, if you were a young man with your eyes watching the waves of her hair you'd have gotten an idea how cliffs, icebergs, and even mountains can be shattered. And wouldn't you want those waves to cascade over you? Yes, sir! . . . I can see myself standing before her as I'm standing before you now. She was lovelier that day than ever, and the look she gave me I'll carry to my grave. That was love. She saw me play Hamlet, and that was enough. I didn't have to court her, or tell any lies. She just loved me. There I was, the promising young actor, and, being filled with rapture and bliss, and a youthful sense of the dramatic, I got down on my knees and begged her to marry me. [*His voice sinks*] And she? . . . She said: 'Give up the theatre!' Give up the theatre! What do you know? She could be madly in love with an actor, but marry one? No, sir! Not on your life! I remember, that night I was playing in . . . well, some stupid comedy, and as I walked through that silly part, my eyes opened. For the first time in my life I realized that anyone who thinks acting is one of the holy arts is an ass! I suddenly saw that it's all lies and nonsense, and that I was a slave, a court fool, a sideshow freak, kept alive to amuse people after work! In short—a clown! Oh, I saw through 'the public' that day! And since then, I don't believe in applause, or reviews, or awards, or 'The, Theatre!' Sure, they'll clap for me, buy my photograph, but when you get down to it, I'm an alien to them, just so much dirt, practically a prostitute. To flatter their ego they'll wangle an introduction to me, buy me a drink, but find one who'd be willing to marry his sister or daughter to me, just try . . .! I don't believe in them! [*Drops on the stool*] I don't believe in them!

NIKITA: You don't look like your old self, Vassily Vassilyitch. You frighten me. How about letting me take you home?

SVETLOVIDOV: I saw through the whole damn business . . . And, believe me, you pay for a vision like that! After that . . . after that girl . . . I didn't care what I did. I just

lived, frittered my life away without a thought for the
future. I acted jokesters, freaks, idiots, the crummiest
parts. I played the fool. I was what's known as a cor-
rupting influence. But, just the same, what an actor I was!
What talent I had! Even if I did waste it. Because that's
what I did, threw it away. My speech got sloppy, I lost
that grace, that power to project a character, authority . . .
This black hole has swallowed me alive! I never knew it
before, but, tonight, when I woke up, I looked back and
there were sixty-eight years behind me. What I'm staring
at is my old age! My song is sung! [*Sobs*] My song is sung!
[*Collapses*]

NIKITA: Come on, Vassily Vassilyitch, try to calm down.
Get a hold on yourself! God help us all! [*Shouting*]
Yegorka! Yegorka!

SVETLOVIDOV: [*Recovering suddenly*] But what talent I had!
Listen, you can't imagine what power, what feeling, what
control, what delivery there is in here! [*Beats his chest*]
Listen, man! Listen to this! Here, let me get my breath.
Remember this, from Marc Antony's great speech?

'Ingratitude, more strong than traitor's arms,
    Quite vanquished him: then burst his mighty heart;
    And, in his mantle muffling up his face,
    Even at the base of Pompey's statua,
    Which all the while ran blood, great Caesar fell.'

Not bad at all, eh? Hang on, here's a little something from
King Lear. You know it. The sky's black, rain,
thunder-rrrr, lightning—tzzzz-ssshh—and then!

'Blow winds, and crack your cheeks! Rage! Blow!
You cataracts and hurricanoes, spout
Till you have drenched our steeples, drowned the
    cocks!
You sulphurous and thought-executing fires,
Vaunt-couriers to oak-cleaving thunderbolts,
Singe my white head! And thou, all-shaking thunder,
Smite flat the thick rotundity of the world!

Crack nature's moulds, all germens spill at once,
That make ingrateful man!'
[*Impatiently*] Come on, quick! The Fool's cue! Give it to
me. I can't wait forever!

NIKITA: [*Acting the Fool*] 'O nuncle, court holy water in a
dry house is better than this rain water out o' door. Good
nuncle, in and ask thy daughter's blessing: here's a night
pities neither wise man nor fool.'

SVETLOVIDOV:

'Rumble thy bellyful! Spit, fire, spout, rain!
Nor wind, rain, thunder, fire are my daughters:
I tax not you, you elements, with unkindness;
I never gave you kingdom, called you children.'

There's power for you! Talent, eh? An actor! Some more,
something from the old days. Let's have a go at—[*Breaks
into a delighted laugh*] Hamlet! Let's see, what'll it be? Yes,
I've got it . . . 'Oh, the recorders! Let me see one. [*To
NIKITA*] Why do you go about as if you would drive me
into a toil?'

NIKITA: 'Oh, my lord, if my duty be too bold, my love is
too unmannerly.'

SVETLOVIDOV: 'I do not well understand that. Will you play
upon this pipe?'

NIKITA: 'My lord, I cannot.'

SVETLOVIDOV: 'I pray you.'

NIKITA: 'Believe me, I cannot.'

SVETLOVIDOV: 'I do beseech you.'

NIKITA: 'I know no touch of it, my lord.'

SVETLOVIDOV: 'Tis as easy as lying: govern these ventages
with your fingers and thumb, give it breath with your
mouth and it will discourse most eloquent music.'

NIKITA: 'I have not the skill.'

SVETLOVIDOV: 'Why, look you now, how unworthy a thing
you make of me! You would play upon me; you would
seem to know my stops; you would pluck out the heart of
my mystery. Do you think I am easier to be played on

than a pipe? Call me what instrument you will, though
you can fret me, yet you cannot play upon me.' [*Laughs
and applauds*] Bravo! Bravo! Where's your old age now?
No old age in that! To hell with old age and all that
tommyrot! I can feel genius flowing through every one of
my veins, and if that isn't youth, and vitality, and life,
what is, I ask you? Where there's talent there's no such
thing as old age, Nikitushka. That's the only truth about
life! That moved you, eh, Nikitushka? Bowled you over?
Why not? Well, that's not all. How's this for tenderness,
delicacy, music . . . Shhh, silence!

'How sweet the moonlight sleeps upon this bank!
Here we will sit, and let the sounds of music
Creep in our ears: soft stillness and the night
Become the touches of sweet harmony.'

[*The sound of doors opening offstage*] What's that?

NIKITA: It must be Yegorka . . . That was genius, Vassily
Vassilyitch, real genius! So help me!

SVETLOVIDOV: [*Turning towards the noise, and shouting*] This
way, me hearty! [*To* NIKITA] There's no such thing as old
age! Whoever started that nonsense anyway? [*Laughs
gaily*] Hey, you're not crying, are you? What for, old man,
what for? What good is that? Come on, now, cut it out!
That's not the way. Come on . . . [*Embraces him, with
tears in his eyes*] Where there's art and genius, there's no
old age, or loneliness, or sickness, and death itself is
robbed of half its terror. [*Sheds a tear*] Yes, Nikitushka,
our song is sung. Hah! Genius, my foot! I'm an empty
bottle, a squeezed-out lemon, a spineless wonder, and you
—you are an old theatre rat, a provincial prompter. Well,
let's go! [*They start off*] You know, I don't have any
talent. About the only thing I'm good for in serious drama
is one of Fortinbras' retinue, and I'm too old even for
that now . . . Sure . . . What do you know? . . . Say, do
you remember that passage from *Othello*, Nikitushka?

'Farewell the tranquil mind! Farewell, content!

Farewell the pluméd troop, and the big wars
That make ambition virtue! Oh, farewell!
Farewell the neighing steed, and the shrill trump,
The spirit-stirring drum, the ear-piercing fife,
The royal banner, and all quality,
Pride, pomp, and circumstance of glorious war!'

NIKITA: Genius, real genius!

SVETLOVIDOV: Or take this: [*Going off*]
'Life's but a walking shadow, a poor player
That struts and frets his hour upon a stage,
And then is heard no more.'
[*Completely offstage by now*]
'A horse! a horse! my kingdom for a horse!'

CURTAIN

The Brute

A JOKE IN ONE ACT
(1888)

ENGLISH VERSION
by ERIC BENTLEY

CHARACTERS

MRS. POPOV, *widow and landowner, small, with dimpled cheeks.*

MR. GRIGORY S. SMIRNOV, *gentleman farmer, middle-aged.*

LUKA, *Mrs. Popov's footman, an old man.*

GARDENER, COACHMAN, HIRED MEN.

The Brute

The drawing room of a country house. MRS. POPOV, *in deep
mourning, is staring hard at a photograph.* LUKA *is with her.*

LUKA: It's not right, ma'am, you're killing yourself. The
cook has gone off with the maid to pick berries. The cat's
having a high old time in the yard catching birds. Every
living thing is happy. But you stay moping here in the
house like it was a convent, taking no pleasure in nothing.
I mean it, ma'am! It must be a full year since you set
foot out of doors.

MRS. POPOV: I must never set foot out of doors again, Luka.
Never! I have nothing to set foot out of doors *for*. My
life is done. *He* is in his grave. I have buried myself alive
in this house. We are *both* in our graves.

LUKA: You're off again, ma'am. I just won't listen to you
no more. Mr. Popov is dead, but what can we do about
that? It's God's doing. God's will be done. You've cried
over him, you've done your share of mourning, haven't
you? There's a limit to everything. You can't go on
weeping and wailing forever. My old lady died, for that
matter, and I wept and wailed over her a whole month
long. Well, that was it. I couldn't weep and wail all my
life, she just wasn't worth it. [*He sighs*] As for the neighbours, you've forgotten all about them, ma'am. You don't
visit them and you don't let them visit you. You and I
are like a pair of spiders—excuse the expression, ma'am—
here we are in this house like a pair of spiders, we never
see the light of day. And it isn't like there was no nice
people around either. The whole county's swarming with
'em. There's a regiment quartered at Riblov, and the
officers are so good-looking! The girls can't take their

eyes off them—There's a ball at the camp every Friday—
The military band plays most every day of the week—
What do you say, ma'am? You're young, you're pretty,
you could enjoy yourself! Ten years from now you may
want to strut and show your feathers to the officers, and
it'll be too late.

MRS. POPOV: [*Firmly*] You must never bring this subject up
again, Luka. Since Popov died, life has been an empty
dream to me, you know that. *You* may think I am alive.
Poor ignorant Luka! You are wrong. I am dead. I'm in
my grave. Never more shall I see the light of day, never
strip from my body this . . . raiment of death! Are you
listening, Luka? Let his ghost learn how I love him! Yes,
I know, and *you* know, he was often unfair to me, he was
cruel to me, and he was unfaithful to me. What of it?
I shall be faithful to *him*, that's all. I will show him how
I can love. Hereafter, in a better world than this, he will
welcome me back, the same loyal girl I always was—

LUKA: Instead of carrying on this way, ma'am, you should
go out in the garden and take a bit of a walk, ma'am. Or
why not harness Toby and take a drive? Call on a couple
of the neighbours, ma'am?

MRS. POPOV: [*Breaking down*] Oh, Luka!

LUKA: Yes, ma'am? What have I said, ma'am? Oh dear!

MRS. POPOV: Toby! You said Toby! He adored that horse.
When he drove me out to the Korchagins and the Vlasovs,
it was always with Toby! He was a wonderful driver, do
you remember, Luka? So graceful! So strong! I can see
him now, pulling at those reins with all his might and
main! Toby! Luka, tell them to give Toby an extra portion
of oats today.

LUKA: Yes, ma'am.

    [*A BELL rings*]

MRS. POPOV: Who is that? Tell them I'm not at home.

LUKA: Very good, ma'am. [*Exit*]

MRS. POPOV: [*Gazing again at the photograph*] You shall see, my Popov, how a wife can love and forgive. Till death do us part. Longer than that. Till death re-unite us forever! [*Suddenly a titter breaks through her tears*] Aren't you ashamed of yourself, Popov? Here's your little wife, being good, being faithful, so faithful she's locked up here waiting for her own funeral, while you—doesn't it make you ashamed, you naughty boy? You were terrible, you know. You were unfaithful, and you made those awful scenes about it, you stormed out and left me alone for weeks—

[*Enter* LUKA]

LUKA: [*Upset*] There's someone asking for you, ma'am. Says he must—

MRS. POPOV: I suppose you told him that since my husband's death I see no one?

LUKA: Yes, ma'am. I did, ma'am. But he wouldn't listen, ma'am. He says it's urgent.

MRS. POPOV: [*Shrilly*] I see no one!!

LUKA: He won't take no for an answer, ma'am. He just curses and swears and comes in anyway. He's a perfect monster, ma'am. He's in the dining room right now.

MRS. POPOV: In the dining room, is he? I'll give him his come uppance. Bring him in here this minute.

[*Exit* LUKA]

[*Suddenly sad again*] Why do they do this to me? Why? Insulting my grief, intruding on my solitude? [*She sighs*] I'm afraid I'll have to enter a convent. I will, I *must* enter a convent!

[*Enter* MR. SMIRNOV *and* LUKA]

SMIRNOV: [*To* LUKA] Dolt! Idiot! You talk too much! [*Seeing* MRS. POPOV. *With dignity*] May I have the honour of introducing myself, madam? Grigory S. Smirnov, landowner and lieutenant of artillery, retired. Forgive me, madam, if I disturb your peace and quiet, but my business is both urgent and weighty.

MRS. POPOV: [*Declining to offer him her hand*] What is it you wish, sir?

SMIRNOV: At the time of his death, your late husband—with whom I had the honour to be acquainted, ma'am—was in my debt to the tune of twelve hundred rubles. I have two notes to prove it. Tomorrow, ma'am, I must pay the interest on a bank loan. I have therefore no alternative, ma'am, but to ask you to pay me the money today.

MRS. POPOV: Twelve hundred rubles? But what did my husband owe it to you for?

SMIRNOV: He used to buy his oats from me, madam.

MRS. POPOV: [*To* LUKA, *with a sigh*] Remember what I said, Luka: tell them to give Toby an extra portion of oats today!

[*Exit* LUKA]

My dear Mr.—what was the name again?

SMIRNOV: Smirnov, ma'am.

MRS. POPOV: My dear Mr. Smirnov, if Mr. Popov owed you money, you shall be paid—to the last ruble, to the last kopeck. But today—you must excuse me, Mr.—what was it?

SMIRNOV: Smirnov, ma'am.

MRS. POPOV: Today, Mr. Smirnov, I have no ready cash in the house.

[SMIRNOV *starts to speak*]

Tomorrow, Mr. Smirnov, no, the day after tomorrow, all will be vell. My steward will be back from town. I shall see that he pays what is owing. Today, no. In any case, today is exactly seven months from Mr. Popov's death. On such a day you will understand that I am in no mood to think of money.

SMIRNOV: Madam, if you don't pay up now, you can carry me out feet foremost. They'll seize my estate.

MRS. POPOV: You can have your money.

[*He starts to thank her*]

Tomorrow.

[*He again starts to speak*]

That is: the day after tomorrow.

SMIRNOV: I don't need the money the day after tomorrow. I need it today.

MRS. POPOV: I'm sorry, Mr.—

SMIRNOV: [*Shouting*] Smirnov!

MRS. POPOV: [*Sweetly*] Yes, of course. But you can't have it today.

SMIRNOV: But I can't wait for it any longer!

MRS. POPOV: Be sensible, Mr. Smirnov. How can I pay you if I don't have it?

SMIRNOV: You don't have it?

MRS. POPOV: I don't have it.

SMIRNOV: Sure?

MRS. POPOV: Positive.

SMIRNOV: Very well. I'll make a note to that effect. [*Shrugging*] And then they want me to keep cool. I meet the tax commissioner on the street, and he says, 'Why are you always in such a bad humour, Smirnov?' Bad humour! How can I help it, in God's name? I need money, I need it desperately. Take yesterday: I leave home at the crack of dawn, I call on all my debtors. Not a one of them pays up. Footsore and weary, I creep at midnight into some little dive, and try to snatch a few winks of sleep on the floor by the vodka barrel. Then today, I come here, fifty miles from home, saying to myself, 'At last, at last, I can be sure of something,' and you're not in the mood! You give me a mood! Christ, how can I help getting all worked up?

MRS. POPOV: I thought I'd made it clear, Mr. Smirnov, that you'll get your money the minute my steward is back from town?

SMIRNOV: What the hell do I care about your steward? Pardon the expression, ma'am. But it was you I came to see.

MRS. POPOV: What language! What a tone to take to a lady! I refuse to hear another word. [*Quickly, exit*]

SMIRNOV: Not in the mood, huh? 'Exactly seven months since Popov's death,' huh? How about me? [*Shouting after her*] Is there this interest to pay, or isn't there? I'm asking you a question: is there this interest to pay, or isn't there? So your husband died, and you're not in the mood, and your steward's gone off some place, and so forth and so on, but what *I* can do about all that, huh? What do *you* think I should do? Take a running jump and shove my head through the wall? Take off in a balloon? You don't know my *other* debtors. I call on Gruzdeff. Not at home. I look for Yaroshevitch. He's hiding out. I find Kooritsin. He kicks up a row, and I have to throw him through the window. I work my way right down the list. Not a kopeck. Then I come to you, and God damn it to hell, if you'll pardon the expression, you're not in the mood! [*Quietly, as he realizes he's talking to air*] I've spoiled them all, that's what, I've let them play me for a sucker. Well, I'll show them. I'll show this one. I'll stay right here till she pays up. Ugh! [*He shudders with rage*] I'm in a rage! I'm in a positively towering rage! Every nerve in my body is trembling at forty to the dozen! I can't breathe, I feel ill, I think I'm going to faint, hey, you there!

[*Enter* LUKA]

LUKA: Yes, sir? Is there anything you wish, sir?

SMIRNOV: Water! Water!! No, make it vodka.

[*Exit* LUKA]

Consider the logic of it. A fellow creature is desperately in need of cash, so desperately in need that he has to seriously contemplate hanging himself, and this woman, this mere chit of a girl, won't pay up, and why not? Because, forsooth, she isn't in the mood! Oh, the logic of women! Come to that, I never have liked them, I could do without the whole sex. Talk to a woman? I'd rather sit on a barrel of dynamite, the very thought gives me gooseflesh. Women! Creatures of poetry and romance! Just to see one in the distance gets me mad. My legs start twitching with rage. I feel like yelling for help.

[*Enter* LUKA, *handing* SMIRNOV *a glass of water*]

LUKA: Mrs. Popov is indisposed, sir. She is seeing no one.
SMIRNOV: Get out.

[*Exit* LUKA]

Indisposed, is she? Seeing no one, huh? Well, she can see
me or not, but I'll be here, I'll be right here till she pays
up. If you're sick for a week, I'll be here for a week. If
you're sick for a year, I'll be here for a year. You won't
get around *me* with your widow's weeds and your school-
girl dimples. I know all about dimples. [*Shouting through
the window*] Semyon, let the horses out of those shafts,
we're not leaving, we're staying, and tell them to give the
horses some oats, yes, oats, you fool, what do you think?
[*Walking away from the window*] What a mess, what an
unholy mess! I didn't sleep last night, the heat is terrific
today, not a damn one of 'em has paid up, and here's
this—this skirt in mourning that's not in the mood! My
head aches, where's that— [*He drinks from the glass*]
Water, ugh! You there!

[*Enter* LUKA]

LUKA: Yes, sir. You wish for something, sir?
SMIRNOV: Where's that confounded vodka I asked for?

[*Exit* LUKA]

[SMIRNOV *sits and looks himself over*] Oof! A fine figure
of a man *I* am! Unwashed, uncombed, unshaven, straw
on my vest, dust all over me. The little woman must've
taken me for a highwayman. [*Yawns*] I suppose it wouldn't
be considered polite to barge into a drawing room in this
state, but who cares? I'm not a visitor, I'm a creditor—
most unwelcome of guests, second only to Death.

[*Enter* LUKA]

LUKA: [*Handing him the vodka*] If I may say so, sir, you take
too many liberties, sir.
SMIRNOV: What?!
LUKA: Oh, nothing, sir, nothing.
SMIRNOV: Who in hell do you think you're talking to? Shut
your mouth!

LUKA: [*Aside*] There's an evil spirit abroad. The Devil must have sent him. Oh! [*Exit* LUKA]

SMIRNOV: What a rage I'm in! I'll grind the whole world to powder. Oh, I feel ill again. You there!

[*Enter* MRS. POPOV]

MRS. POPOV: [*Looking at the floor*] In the solitude of my rural retreat, Mr. Smirnov, I've long since grown unaccustomed to the sound of the human voice. Above all, I cannot bear shouting. I must beg you not to break the silence.

SMIRNOV: Very well. Pay me my money and I'll go.

MRS. POPOV: I told you before, and I tell you again, Mr. Smirnov: I have no cash, you'll have to wait till the day after tomorrow. Can I express myself more plainly?

SMIRNOV: And *I* told *you* before, and *I* tell *you* again, that I need the money today, that the day after tomorrow is too late, and that if you don't pay, and pay now, I'll have to hang myself in the morning!

MRS. POPOV: But I have no cash. This is quite a puzzle.

SMIRNOV: You won't pay, huh?

MRS. POPOV: I *can't* pay, Mr. Smirnov.

SMIRNOV: In that case, I'm going to sit here and wait. [*Sits down*] You'll pay up the day after tomorrow? Very good. Till the day after tomorrow, here I sit. [*Pause. He jumps up*] Now look, do I have to pay that interest tomorrow, or don't I? Or do you think I'm joking?

MRS. POPOV: I must ask you not to raise your voice, Mr. Smirnov. This is not a stable.

SMIRNOV: Who said it was? Do I have to pay the interest tomorrow or not?

MRS. POPOV: Mr. Smirnov, do you know how to behave in the presence of a lady?

SMIRNOV: No, madam, I do not know how to behave in the presence of a lady.

MRS. POPOV: Just what I thought. I look at you, and I say: ugh! I hear you talk, and I say to myself: 'That man doesn't know how to talk to a lady.'

SMIRNOV: You'd like me to come simpering to you in French, I suppose. '*Enchanté, madame! Merci beaucoup* for not paying zee money, *madame! Pardonnez-moi* if I 'ave disturbed you, *madame!* How *charmante* you look in mourning, *madame!*'

MRS. POPOV: Now you're being silly, Mr. Smirnov.

SMIRNOV: [*Mimicking*] 'Now you're being silly, Mr. Smirnov.' 'You don't know how to talk to a lady, Mr. Smirnov.' Look here, Mrs. Popov, I've known more women than you've known pussy cats. I've fought three duels on their account. I've jilted twelve, and been jilted by nine others. Oh, yes, Mrs. Popov, I've played the fool in my time, whispered sweet nothings, bowed and scraped and endeavoured to please. Don't tell me I don't know what it is to love, to pine away with longing, to have the blues, to melt like butter, to be weak as water. I was full of tender emotion. I was carried away with passion. I squandered half my fortune on the sex. I chattered about women's emancipation. But there's an end to everything, dear madam. Burning eyes, dark eyelashes, ripe, red lips, dimpled cheeks, heaving bosoms, soft whisperings, the moon above, the lake below—I don't give a rap for that sort of nonsense any more, Mrs. Popov. I've found out about women. Present company excepted, they're liars. Their behaviour is mere play acting; their conversation is sheer gossip. Yes, dear lady, women, young or old, are false, petty, vain, cruel, malicious unreasonable. As for intelligence, any sparrow could give them points. Appearances, I admit, can be deceptive. In appearance, a woman may be all poetry and romance, goddess and angel, muslin and fluff. To look at her exterior is to be transported to heaven. But I have looked at her interior, Mrs. Popov, and what did I find there—in her very soul? A crocodile. [*He has gripped the back of the chair so firmly that it snaps*] And, what is more revolting, a crocodile with an illusion, a crocodile that imagines tender sentiments are its own special province, a crocodile that thinks itself queen of the realm of love! Whereas, in sober fact, dear madam, if a woman can love anything except a lapdog you can hang me by the feet on that nail. For a man, love is suffering, love is sacrifice. A woman just swishes her train around and tightens her grip on your nose. Now, you're a woman, aren't you, Mrs. Popov? You must be an expert on some of this. Tell me, quite frankly, did you ever know a woman to be—faithful, for instance? Or even sincere? Only old hags, huh? Though some women are old hags from birth. But as for the others? You're right: a faithful woman is a freak of nature —like a cat with horns.

MRS. POPOV: Who *is* faithful, then? Who *have* you cast for the faithful lover? Not man?

SMIRNOV: Right first time, Mrs. Popov: man.

MRS. POPOV: [*Going off into a peal of bitter laughter*] Man! Man is faithful! That's a new one! [*Fiercely*] What right do you have to say this, Mr. Smirnov? Men faithful? Let me tell you something. Of all the men I have ever known my late husband Popov was the best. I loved him, and there are women who know how to love, Mr. Smirnov. I gave him my youth, my happiness, my life, my fortune. I worshipped the ground he trod on—and what happened? The best of men was unfaithful to me, Mr. Smirnov. Not once in a while. All the time. After he died, I found his desk drawer full of love letters. While he was alive, he was always going away for the week-end. He squandered my money. He made love to other women before my very eyes. But, in spite of all, Mr. Smirnov, *I* was faithful. Unto death. And beyond. I am *still* faithful, Mr. Smirnov! Buried alive in this house, I shall wear mourning till the day I, too, am called to my eternal rest.

SMIRNOV: [*Laughing scornfully*] Expect me to believe that? As if I couldn't see through all this hocus-pocus. Buried alive! Till you're called to your eternal rest! Till when?

Till some little poet—or some little subaltern with his first moustache—comes riding by and asks: 'Can that be the house of the mysterious Tamara who for love of her late husband has buried herself alive, vowing to see no man?' Ha!

MRS. POPOV: [*Flaring up*] How dare you? How dare you insinuate—?

SMIRNOV: You may have buried yourself alive, Mrs. Popov, but you haven't forgotten to powder your nose.

MRS. POPOV: [*Incoherent*] How dare you? How—?

SMIRNOV: Who's raising his voice now? Just because I call a spade a spade. Because I shoot straight from the shoulder. Well, don't shout at me, I'm not your steward.

MRS. POPOV: I'm not shouting, you're shouting! Oh, leave me alone!

SMIRNOV: Pay me the money, and I will.

MRS. POPOV: You'll get no money out of me!

SMIRNOV: Oh, so that's it!

MRS. POPOV: Not a ruble, not a kopeck. Get out! Leave me alone!

SMIRNOV: Not being your husband, I must ask you not to make scenes with me. [*He sits*] I don't like scenes.

MRS. POPOV: [*Choking with rage*] You're sitting down?

SMIRNOV: Correct, I'm sitting down.

MRS. POPOV: I asked you to leave!

SMIRNOV: Then give me the money. [*Aside*] Oh, what a rage I'm in, what a rage!

MRS. POPOV: The impudence of the man! I won't talk to you a moment longer. Get out. [*Pause*] Are you going?

SMIRNOV: No.

MRS. POPOV: No?!

SMIRNOV: No.

MRS. POPOV: On your head be it. Luka!
    [*Enter* LUKA]
Show the gentleman out, Luka.

LUKA: [*Approaching*] I'm afraid, sir, I'll have to ask you, um, to leave, sir, now, um—

SMIRNOV: [*Jumping up*] Shut your mouth, you old idiot! Who do you think you're talking to? I'll make mincemeat of you.

LUKA: [*Clutching his heart*] Mercy on us! Holy saints above! [*He falls into an armchair*] I'm taken sick! I can't breathe!!

MRS. POPOV: Then where's Dasha? Dasha! Dasha! Come here at once! [*She rings*]

LUKA: They gone picking berries, ma'am, I'm alone here—Water, water, I'm taken sick!

MRS. POPOV: [*To* SMIRNOV] Get out, you!

SMIRNOV: Can't you even be polite with me, Mrs. Popov?

MRS. POPOV: [*Clenching her fists and stamping her feet*] With you? You're a wild animal, you were never house-broken!

SMIRNOV: What? What did you say?

MRS. POPOV: I said you were a wild animal, you were never house-broken.

SMIRNOV: [*Advancing upon her*] And what right do you have to talk to me like that?

MRS. POPOV: Like what?

SMIRNOV: You have insulted me, madam.

MRS. POPOV: What of it? Do you think I'm scared of you?

SMIRNOV: So you think you can get away with it because you're a woman. A creature of poetry and romance, huh? Well, it doesn't go down with me. I hereby challenge you to a duel.

LUKA: Mercy on us! Holy saints alive! Water!

SMIRNOV: I propose we shoot it out.

MRS. POPOV: Trying to scare me again? Just because you have big fists and a voice like a bull? You're a brute.

SMIRNOV: No one insults Grigory S. Smirnov with impunity! And I don't care if you *are* a female.

MRS. POPOV: [*Trying to outshout him*] Brute, brute, brute!

SMIRNOV: The sexes are equal, are they? Fine: then it's just prejudice to expect men alone to pay for insults. I hereby challenge—

MRS. POPOV: [*Screaming*] All right! You want to shoot it out? All right! Let's shoot it out!

SMIRNOV: And let it be here and now!

MRS. POPOV: Here and now! All right! I'll have Popov's
pistols here in one minute! [*Walks away, then turns*]
Putting one of Popov's bullets through your silly head will
be a pleasure! Au revoir. [*Exit*]

SMIRNOV: I'll bring her down like a duck, a sitting duck.
I'm not one of your little poets, I'm no little subaltern with
his first moustache. No, sir, there's no weaker sex where
I'm concerned!

LUKA: Sir! Master! [*He goes down on his knees*] Take pity
on a poor old man, and do me a favour: go away. It was
bad enough before, you nearly scared me to death. But a
duel—!

SMIRNOV: [*Ignoring him*] A duel! That's equality of the sexes
for you! That's women's emancipation! Just as a matter
of principle I'll bring her down like a duck. But what a
woman! 'Putting one of Popov's bullets through your silly
head . . .' Her cheeks were flushed, her eyes were gleaming!
And, by God, she's accepted the challenge! I never knew
a woman like this before!

LUKA: Sir! Master! Please go away! I'll always pray for
you!

SMIRNOV: [*Again ignoring him*] What a woman! Phew!!
She's no sour puss, *she's* no cry baby. She's fire and brim-
stone. She's a human cannon ball. What a shame I have
to kill her!

LUKA: [*Weeping*] Please, kind sir, please, go away!

SMIRNOV: [*As before*] I like her, isn't that funny? With those
dimples and all? I like her. I'm even prepared to consider
letting her off that debt. And where's my rage? It's gone.
I never knew a woman like this before.

[*Enter* MRS. POPOV *with pistols*]

MRS. POPOV: [*Boldly*] Pistols, Mr. Smirnov! [*Matter of fact*]
But before we start, you'd better show me how it's done,
I'm not too familiar with these things. In fact I never gave
a pistol a second look.

LUKA: Lord, have mercy on us, I must go hunt up the gardener and the coachman. Why has this catastrophe fallen upon us, O Lord? [*Exit*]

SMIRNOV: [*Examining the pistols*] Well, it's like this. There are several makes: one is the Mortimer, with capsules, especially constructed for duelling. What you have here are Smith and Wesson triple-action revolvers, with extractor, first-rate job, worth ninety rubles at the very least. You hold it this way. [*Aside*] My God, what eyes she has! They're setting me on fire.

MRS. POPOV: This way?

SMIRNOV: Yes, that's right. You cock the trigger, take aim like this, head up, arm out like this. Then you just press with this finger here, and it's all over. The main thing is, keep cool, take slow aim, and don't let your arm jump.

MRS. POPOV: I see. And if it's inconvenient to do the job here, we can go out in the garden.

SMIRNOV: Very good. Of course, I should warn you: I'll be firing in the air.

MRS. POPOV: What? This is the end. Why?

SMIRNOV: Oh, well—because—for private reasons.

MRS. POPOV: Scared, huh? [*She laughs heartily*] Now don't you try to get out of it, Mr. Smirnov. My blood is up. I won't be happy till I've drilled a hole through that skull of yours. Follow me. What's the matter? Scared?

SMIRNOV: That's right. I'm scared.

MRS. POPOV: Oh, come on, what's the matter with you?

SMIRNOV: Well, um, Mrs. Popov, I, um, I like you.

MRS. POPOV: [*Laughing bitterly*] Good God! He likes me, does he? The gall of the man. [*Showing him the door*] You may leave, Mr. Smirnov.

SMIRNOV: [*Quietly puts the gun down, takes his hat, and walks to the door. Then he stops and the pair look at each other without a word. Then, approaching gingerly*] Listen, Mrs. Popov. Are you still mad at me? I'm in the devil of a temper myself, of course. But then, you see—what I mean is—it's this way—the fact is—[*Roaring*] Well, is it my fault, damn it, if I like you. [*Clutches the back of a chair. It breaks*] Christ, what fragile furniture you have here. I like you. Know what I mean? I could fall in love with you.

MRS. POPOV: I hate you. Get out!

SMIRNOV: What a woman! I never saw anything like it. Oh, I'm lost, I'm done for, I'm a mouse in a trap.

MRS. POPOV: Leave this house, or I shoot!

SMIRNOV: Shoot away! What bliss to die of a shot that was fired by that little velvet hand! To die gazing into those enchanting eyes. I'm out of my mind. I know: you must decide at once. Think for one second, then decide. Because if I leave now, I'll never be back. Decide! I'm a pretty decent chap. Landed gentleman, I should say. Ten thousand a year. Good stable. Throw a kopeck up in the air, and I'll put a bullet through it. Will you marry me?

MRS. POPOV: [*Indignant, brandishing the gun*] We'll shoot it out! Get going! Take your pistol!

SMIRNOV: I'm out of my mind. I don't understand anything any more. [*Shouting*] You there! That vodka!

MRS. POPOV: No excuses! No delays! We'll shoot it out!

SMIRNOV: I'm out of my mind. I'm falling in love. I *have* fallen in love. [*He takes her hand vigorously; she squeals*] I love you. [*He goes down on his knees*] I love you as I've never loved before. I jilted twelve, and was jilted by nine others. But I didn't love a one of them as I love you. I'm full of tender emotion. I'm melting like butter. I'm weak as water. I'm on my knees like a fool, and I offer you my hand. It's a shame, it's a disgrace. I haven't been in love in five years. I took a vow against it. And now, all of a sudden, to be swept off my feet, it's a scandal. I offer you my hand, dear lady. Will you or won't you? You won't? Then don't! [*He rises and walks toward the door*]

MRS. POPOV: I didn't say anything.

SMIRNOV: [*Stopping*] What?

MRS. POPOV: Oh, nothing, you can go. Well, no, just a minute. No, you can go. Go! I detest you! But, just a moment. Oh, if you knew how furious I feel! [*Throws the gun on the table*] My fingers have gone to sleep holding that horrid thing. [*She is tearing her handkerchief to shreds*] And what are you standing around for? Get out of here!

SMIRNOV: Goodbye.

MRS. POPOV: Go, go, go! [*Shouting*] Where are you going? Wait a minute! No, no, it's all right, just go. I'm fighting mad. Don't come near me, don't come near me!

SMIRNOV: [*Who IS coming near her*] I'm pretty disgusted with myself—falling in love like a kid, going down on my knees like some moongazing whippersnapper, the very thought gives me gooseflesh. [*Rudely*] I love you. But it doesn't make sense. Tomorrow, I have to pay that interest, and we've already started mowing. [*He puts his arm about her waist*] I shall never forgive myself for this.

MRS. POPOV: Take your hands off me, I hate you! Let's shoot it out!

[*A long kiss. Enter* LUKA *with an axe, the* GARDENER *with a rake, the* COACHMAN *with a pitchfork,* HIRE MEN *with sticks*]

LUKA: [*Seeing the kiss*] Mercy on us! Holy saints above!

MRS. POPOV: [*Dropping her eyes*] Luka, tell them in the stable that Toby is *not* to have any oats today.

CURTAIN

A Marriage Proposal

A JOKE IN ONE ACT
(1888–1889)

ENGLISH VERSION
by THEODORE HOFFMAN

CHARACTERS

STEPAN STEPANOVITCH CHUBUKOV, *a landowner, elderly, pompous but affable.*

IVAN VASSILEVITCH LOMOV, *healthy, but a hypochondriac; nervous, suspicious. Also a landowner*

NATALIA STEPANOVNA, *Chubukov's daughter; twenty-five but still unmarried.*

A Marriage Proposal

Chubukov's mansion—the living room.

LOMOV *enters, formally dressed in evening jacket, white gloves, top hat. He is nervous from the start.*

CHUBUKOV: [*Rising*] Well, look who's here! Ivan Vassilevitch! [*Shakes his hand warmly*] What a surprise, old man! How are you?

LOMOV: Oh, not too bad. And you?

CHUBUKOV: Oh, we manage, we manage. Do sit down, please. You know, you've been neglecting your neighbours, my dear fellow. It's been ages. Say, why the formal dress? Tails, gloves, and so forth. Where's the funeral, my boy? Where are you headed?

LOMOV: Oh, nowhere. I mean, here; just to see you, my dear Stepan Stepanovitch.

CHUBUKOV: Then why the full dress, old boy? It's not New Year's, and so forth.

LOMOV: Well, you see, it's like this. I have come here, my dear Stepan Stepanovitch, to bother you with a request. More than once, or twice, or more than that, it has been my privilege to apply to you for assistance in things, and you've always, well, responded. I mean, well, you have. Yes. Excuse me, I'm getting all mixed up. May I have a glass of water, my dear Stepan Stepanovitch? [*Drinks*]

CHUBUKOV: [*Aside*] Wants to borrow some money. Not a chance! [*Aloud*] What can I do for you my dear friend?

LOMOV: Well, you see, my dear Stepanitch . . . Excuse me, I mean Stepan my Dearovitch . . . No, I mean, I get all confused, as you can see. To make a long story short, you're the only one who can help me. Of course, I don't

41

deserve it, and there's no reason why I should expect you
to, and all that.

CHUBUKOV: Stop beating around the bush! Out with it!

LOMOV: In just a minute. I mean, now, right now. The
truth is, I have come to ask the hand . . . I mean, your
daughter, Natalia Stepanovna, I, I want to marry her!

CHUBUKOV: [*Overjoyed*] Great heavens! Ivan Vassilevitch!
Say it again!

LOMOV: I have come humbly to ask for the hand . . .

CHUBUKOV: [*Interrupting*] You're a prince! I'm overwhelmed,
delighted, and so forth. Yes, indeed, and all that! [*Hugs
and kisses* LOMOV] This is just what I've been hoping for.
It's my fondest dream come true. [*Sheds a tear*] And, you
know, I've always looked upon you, my boy, as if you
were my own son. May God grant to both of you His
Mercy and His Love, and so forth. Oh, I have been
wishing for this . . . But why am I being so idiotic? It's
just that I'm off my rocker with joy, my boy! Completely
off my rocker! Oh, with all my soul I'm . . . I'll go get
Natalia, and so forth.

LOMOV: [*Deeply moved*] Dear Stepan Stepanovitch, do you
think she'll agree?

CHUBUKOV: Why, of course, old friend. Great heavens! As
if she wouldn't! Why she's crazy for you! Good God!
Like a love-sick cat, and so forth. Be right back. [*Leaves*]

LOMOV: God, it's cold. I'm gooseflesh all over, as if I had
to take a test. But the main thing is, to make up my mind,
and keep it that way. I mean, if I take time out to think,
or if I hesitate, or talk about it, or have ideals, or wait
for real love, well, I'll just never get married! Brrrr, it's
cold! Natalia Stepanovna is an excellent housekeeper.
She's not too bad looking. She's had a good education.
What more could I ask? Nothing. I'm so nervous, my
ears are buzzing. [*Drinks*] Besides, I've just got to get
married. I'm thirty-five already. It's sort of a critical age.
I've got to settle down and lead a regular life. I mean, I'm

always getting palpitations, and I'm nervous, and I get upset so easy. Look, my lips are quivering, and my eyebrow's twitching. The worst thing is the night. Sleeping. I get into bed, doze off, and, suddenly, something inside me jumps. First my head snaps, and then my shoulder blade, and I roll out of bed like a lunatic and try to walk it off. Then I try to go back to sleep, but, as soon as I do, something jumps again! Twenty times a night, sometimes . . . [*Natalia Stepanovna enters*]

NATALIA: Oh, it's only you. All Papa said was: 'Go inside, there's a merchant come to collect his goods.' How do you do, Ivan Vassilevitch?

LOMOV: How do you do, dear Natalia Stepanovna?

NATALIA: Excuse my apron, and not being dressed. We're shelling peas. You haven't been around lately. Oh, do sit down. [*They do*] Would you like some lunch?

LOMOV: No thanks, I had some.

NATALIA: Well, then smoke if you want. [*He doesn't*] The weather's nice today . . . but yesterday, it was so wet the workmen couldn't get a thing done. Have you got much hay in? I felt so greedy I had a whole field done, but now I'm not sure I was right. With the rain it could rot, couldn't it? I should have waited. But why are you so dressed up? Is there a dance or something? Of course, I must say you look splendid, but . . . Well, tell me, why are you so dressed up?

LOMOV: [*Excited*] Well, you see, my dear Natalia Stepanovna, the truth is, I made up my mind to ask you to . . . well, to, listen to me. Of course, it'll probably surprise you and even maybe make you angry, but . . . [*Aside*] God's it's cold in here!

NATALIA: Why, what do you mean? [*A pause*] Well?

LOMOV: I'll try to get it over with. I mean, you know, my dear Natalia Stepanovna that I've known, since childhood, even, known, and had the privilege of knowing, your family. My late aunt, and her husband, who, as you know, left me my estate, they always had the greatest respect for your father, and your late mother. The Lomovs and the Chubukovs have always been very friendly, you might even say affectionate. And, of course, you know, our land borders on each other's. My Oxen Meadows touch your birch grove . . .

NATALIA: I hate to interrupt you, my dear Ivan Vassilevitch, but you said: 'my Oxen Meadows.' Do you really think they're yours?

LOMOV: Why of course they're mine.

NATALIA: What do you mean? The Oxen Meadows are ours, not yours!

LOMOV: Oh, no, my dear Natalia Stepanovna, they're mine.

NATALIA: Well, this is the first I've heard about it! Where did you get that idea?

LOMOV: Where? Why, I mean the Oxen Meadows that are wedged between your birches and the marsh.

NATALIA: Yes, of course, they're ours.

LOMOV: Oh, no, you're wrong, my dear Natalia Stepanovna, they're mine.

NATALIA: Now, come, Ivan Vassilevitch! How long have they been yours?

LOMOV: How long? Why, as long as I can remember!

NATALIA: Well, really, you can't expect me to believe that!

LOMOV: But, you can see for yourself in the deed, my dear Natalia Stepanovna. Of course, there was once a dispute about them, but everyone knows they're mine now. There's nothing to argue about. There was a time when my aunt's grandmother let your father's grandfather's peasants use the land, but they were supposed to bake bricks for her in return. Naturally, after a few years they began to act as if they owned it, but the real truth is . . .

NATALIA: That has nothing to do with the case! Both my grandfather and my great-grandfather said that their land went as far as the marsh, which means that the Meadows are ours! There's nothing whatever to argue about. It's foolish.

Lomov: But I can show you the deed, Natalia Stepanovna.

Natalia: You're just making fun of me . . . Great Heavens! Here we have the land for hundreds of years, and suddenly you try to tell us it isn't ours. What's wrong with you, Ivan Vassilevitch? Those meadows aren't even fifteen acres, and they're not worth three hundred rubles, but I just can't stand unfairness! I just can't stand unfairness!

Lomov: But, you must listen to me. Your father's grandfather's peasants, as I've already tried to tell you, they were supposed to bake bricks for my aunt's grandmother. And my aunt's grandmother, why, she wanted to be nice to them . . .

Natalia: It's just nonsense, this whole business about aunts and grandfathers and grandmothers. The Meadows are ours! That's all there is to it!

Lomov: They're mine!

Natalia: Ours! You can go on talking for two days, and you can put on fifteen evening coats and twenty pairs of gloves, but I tell you they're ours, ours, ours!

Lomov: Natalia Stepanovna, I don't want the Meadows! I'm just acting on principle. If you want, I'll give them to you.

Natalia: I'll give them to *you*! Because they're ours! And that's all there is to it! And if I may say so, your behaviour, my dear Ivan Vassilevitch, is very strange. Until now, we've always considered you a good neighbour, even a friend. After all, last year we lent you our threshing machine, even though it meant putting off our own threshing until November. And here you are treating us like a pack of gypsies. Giving me my own land, indeed! Really! Why that's not being a good neighbour. It's sheer impudence, that's what it is . . .

Lomov: Oh, so you think I'm just a land-grabber? My dear lady, I've never grabbed anybody's land in my whole life, and no-one's going to accuse me of doing it now! [*Quickly walks over to the pitcher and drinks some more water*] The Oxen Meadows are mine!

NATALIA: That's a lie. They're ours!

LOMOV: Mine!

NATALIA: A lie! I'll prove it. I'll send my mowers out there today!

LOMOV: What?

NATALIA: My mowers will mow it today!

LOMOV: I'll kick them out!

NATALIA: You just dare!

LOMOV: [*Clutching his heart*] The Oxen Meadows are mine! Do you understand? Mine!

NATALIA: Please don't shout! You can shout all you want in your own house, but here I must ask you to control yourself.

LOMOV: If my heart wasn't palpitating the way it is, if my insides weren't jumping like mad, I wouldn't talk to you so calmly. [*Yelling*] The Oxen Meadows are mine!

NATALIA: Ours!

LOMOV: Mine!

NATALIA: Ours!

LOMOV: Mine!

    [*Enter* CHUBUKOV]

CHUBUKOV: What's going on? Why all the shouting?

NATALIA: Papa, will you please inform this gentleman who owns the Oxen Meadows, he or we?

CHUBUKOV: [*To* LOMOV] Why, they're ours, old fellow.

LOMOV: But how can they be yours, my dear Stepan Stepanovitch? Be fair. Perhaps my aunt's grandmother did let your grandfather's peasants work the land, and maybe they did get so used to it that they acted as if it was their own, but . . .

CHUBUKOV: Oh, no, no . . . my dear boy. You forget something. The reason the peasants didn't pay your aunt's grandmother, and so forth, was that the land was disputed, even then. Since then it's been settled. Why, everyone knows it's ours.

LOMOV: I can prove it's mine.

CHUBUKOV: You can't prove a thing, old boy.

LOMOV: Yes I can!

CHUBUKOV: My dear lad, why yell like that? Yelling doesn't prove a thing. Look, I'm not after anything of yours, just as I don't intend to give up anything of mine. Why should I? Besides, if you're going to keep arguing about it, I'd just as soon give the land to the peasants, so there!

LOMOV: There nothing! Where do you get the right to give away someone else's property?

CHUBUKOV: I certainly ought to know if I have the right or not. And you had better realize it, because, my dear young man, I am not used to being spoken to in that tone of voice, and so forth. Besides which, my dear young man, I am twice as old as you are, and I ask you to speak to me without getting yourself into such a tizzy, and so forth!

LOMOV: Do you think I'm a fool? First you call my property yours, and then you expect me to keep calm and polite! Good neighbours don't act like that, my dear Stepan Stepanovitch. You're no neighbour, you're a land grabber!

CHUBUKOV: What was that? What did you say?

NATALIA: Papa, send the mowers out to the meadows at once!

CHUBUKOV: What did you say, sir?

NATALIA: The Oxen Meadows are ours, and we'll never give them up, never, never, never, never!

LOMOV: We'll see about that. I'll go to court. I'll show you!

CHUBUKOV: Go to court? Well, go to court, and so forth! I know you, just waiting for a chance to go to court, and so forth. You pettifogging shyster, you! All of your family is like that. The whole bunch of them!

LOMOV: You leave my family out of this! The Lomovs have always been honourable, upstanding people, and not a one of them was ever tried for embezzlement, like your grandfather was.

CHUBUKOV: The Lomovs are a pack of lunatics, the whole bunch of them!

NATALIA: The whole bunch!

CHUBUKOV: Your grandfather was a drunkard, and what about your other aunt, the one who ran away with the architect? And so forth.

NATALIA: And so forth!

LOMOV: Your mother was a hunch back! [*Clutches at his heart*] Oh, I've got a stitch in my side . . . My head's whirling . . . Help! Water!

CHUBUKOV: Your father was a rum-soaked gambler.

NATALIA: And your aunt was queen of the scandalmongers!

LOMOV: My left foot's paralyzed. You're a plotter . . . Oh, my heart. It's an open secret that in the last elections you brib . . . I'm seeing stars! Where's my hat?

NATALIA: It's a low-mean, spiteful . . .

CHUBUKOV: And you're a two-faced, malicious schemer!

LOMOV: Here's my hat . . . Oh, my heart . . . Where's the door? How do I get out of here? . . . Oh, I think I'm going to die . . . My foot's numb. [*Goes*]

CHUBUKOV [*Following him*] And don't you ever set foot in my house again!

NATALIA: Go to court, indeed! We'll see about that!
[LOMOV *staggers out*]

CHUBUKOV: The devil with him! [*Gets a drink, walks back and forth excited*]

NATALIA: What a rascal! How can you trust your neighbours after an incident like that?

CHUBUKOV: The villain! The scarecrow!

NATALIA: He's a monster! First he tries to steal our land, and then he has the nerve to yell at you.

CHUBUKOV: Yes, and that turnip, that stupid rooster, has the gall to make a proposal. Some proposal!

NATALIA: What proposal?

CHUBUKOV: Why, he came to propose to you.

NATALIA: To propose? To me? Why didn't you tell me before?

CHUBUKOV: So he gets all dressed up in his formal clothes. That stuffed sausage, that dried up cabbage!

NATALIA: To propose to me? Ohhhh! [*Falls into a chair and starts wailing*] Bring him back! Back! Go get him! Bring him back! Ohhhh!

CHUBUKOV: Bring who back?

NATALIA: Hurry up, hurry up! I'm sick. Get him! [*Complete hysterics*]

CHUBUKOV: What for? [*To her*] What's the matter with you? [*Clutches his head*] Oh, what a fool I am! I'll shoot myself! I'll hang myself! I ruined her chances!

NATALIA: I'm dying. Get him!

CHUBUKOV: All right, all right, right away! Only don't yell! [*He runs out*]

NATALIA: What are they doing to me? Get him! Bring him back! Bring him back!

[*A pause.* CHUBUKOV *runs in*]

CHUBUKOV: He's coming, and so forth, the snake. Oof! You talk to him. I'm not in the mood.

NATALIA: [*Wailing*] Bring him back! Bring him back!

CHUBUKOV: [*Yelling*] I told you, he's coming! Oh Lord, what agony to be the father of a grown-up daughter. I'll cut my throat some day, I swear I will. [*To her*] We cursed him, we insulted him, abused him, kicked him out, and now . . . because you, you . . .

NATALIA: Me? It was all your fault!

CHUBUKOV: My fault? What do you mean my fau . . ? [LOMOV *appears in the doorway*] Talk to him yourself! [*Goes out.* LOMOV *enters, exhausted*]

LOMOV: What palpitations! My heart! And my foot's absolutely asleep. Something keeps giving me a stitch in the side . . .

NATALIA: You must forgive us, Ivan Vassilevitch. We all got too excited. I remember now. The Oxen Meadows are yours.

LOMOV: My heart's beating something awful. My Meadows. My eyebrows, they're both twitching!

NATALIA: Yes, the Meadows are all yours, yes, yours. Do sit down. [*They sit*] We were wrong, of course.

LOMOV: I argued on principle. My land isn't worth so much to me, but the principle . . .

NATALIA: Oh, yes, of course, the principle, that's what counts. But let's change the subject.

LOMOV: Besides, I have evidence. You see, my aunt's grandmother let your father's grandfather's peasants use the land . . .

NATALIA: Yes, yes, yes, but forget all that. [*Aside*] I wish I knew how to get him going. [*Aloud*] Are you going to start hunting soon?

LOMOV: After the harvest I'll try for grouse. But oh, my dear Natalia Stepanovna, have you heard about the bad luck I've had? You know my dog, Guess? He's gone lame.

NATALIA: What a pity. Why?

LOMOV: I don't know. He must have twisted his leg, or got in a fight, or something. [*Sighs*] My best dog, to say nothing of the cost. I paid Mironov 125 rubles for him.

NATALIA: That was too high, Ivan Vassilevitch.

LOMOV: I think it was quite cheap. He's a first class dog.

NATALIA: Why Papa only paid 85 rubles for Squeezer, and he's much better than Guess.

LOMOV: Squeezer better than Guess! What an idea! [*Laughs*] Squeezer better than Guess!

NATALIA: Of course he's better. He may still be too young but on points and pedigree, he's a better dog even than any Volchanetsky owns.

LOMOV: Excuse me, Natalia Stepanovna, but you're forgetting he's overshot, and overshot dogs are bad hunters.

NATALIA: Oh, so he's overshot, is he? Well, this is the first time I've heard about it.

LOMOV: Believe me, his lower jaw is shorter than his upper.

NATALIA: You've measured them?

LOMOV: Yes. He's all right for pointing, but if you want him to retrieve . . .

NATALIA: In the first place, our Squeezer is a thoroughbred, the son of Harness and Chisel, while your mutt doesn't even have a pedigree. He's as old and worn out as a pedlar's horse.

LOMOV: He may be old, but I wouldn't take five Squeezers for him. How can you argue? Guess is a dog, Squeezer's a laugh. Anyone you can name has a dog like Squeezer hanging around somewhere. They're under every bush. If he only cost twenty-five rubles you got cheated.

NATALIA: The devil is in you today, Ivan Vassilevitch! You want to contradict everything. First you pretend the Oxen Meadows are yours, and now you say Guess is better than Squeezer. People should say what they really mean, and you know Squeezer is a hundred times better than Guess. Why say he isn't?

LOMOV: So, you think I'm a fool or a blind man, Natalia Stepanovna! Once and for all, Squeezer is overshot!

NATALIA: He is not!

LOMOV: He is so!

NATALIA: He is not!

LOMOV: Why shout, my dear lady?

NATALIA: Why talk such nonsense? It's terrible. Your Guess is old enough to be buried, and you compare him with Squeezer!

LOMOV: I'm sorry, I can't go on. My heart . . . it's palpitating!

NATALIA: I've always noticed that the hunters who argue most don't know a thing.

LOMOV: Please! Be quiet a moment. My heart's falling apart . . . [Shouts] Shut up!

NATALIA: I'm not going to shut up until you admit that Squeezer's a hundred times better than Guess.

LOMOV: A hundred times worse! His head . . . My eyes . . . shoulder . . .

NATALIA: Guess is half-dead already!

LOMOV: [Weeping] Shut up! My heart's exploding!

NATALIA: I won't shut up!

[CHUBUKOV comes in]

CHUBUKOV: What's the trouble now?

NATALIA: Papa, will you please tell us which is the better dog, his Guess or our Squeezer?

LOMOV: Stepan Stepanovitch, I implore you to tell me just one thing; Is your Squeezer overshot or not? Yes or no?

CHUBUKOV: Well what if he is? He's still the best dog in the neighbourhood, and so forth.

LOMOV: Oh, but isn't my dog, Guess, better? Really?

CHUBUKOV: Don't get yourself so fraught up, old man. Of course, your dog has his good points—thorough-bred, firm on his feet, well sprung ribs, and so forth, But, my dear fellow, you've got to admit he has two defects; he's old and he's short in the muzzle.

LOMOV: Short in the muzzle? Oh, my heart! Let's look at the facts! On the Marusinsky hunt my dog ran neck and neck with the Count's, while Squeezer was a mile behind them . . .

CHUBUKOV: That's because the Count's groom hit him with a whip.

LOMOV: And he was right, too! We were fox hunting; what was your dog chasing sheep for?

CHUBUKOV: That's a lie! Look, I'm going to lose my temper . . . [Controlling himself] my dear friend, so let's stop arguing, for that reason alone. You're only arguing because we're all jealous of somebody else's dog. Who can help it? As soon as you realize some dog is better than yours, in this case our dog, you start in with this and that, and the next thing you know—pure jealousy! I remember the whole business.

LOMOV: I remember too!

CHUBUKOV: [Mimicking] 'I remember too!' What do you remember?

LOMOV: My heart . . . my foot's asleep . . . I can't . . .

NATALIA: [Mimicking] 'My heart . . . my foot's asleep.' What kind of a hunter are you? You should be hunting cockroaches in the kitchen, not foxes. 'My heart!'

CHUBUKOV: Yes, what kind of a hunter are you anyway? You should be sitting at home with your palpitations, not tracking down animals. You don't hunt anyhow. You just go out to argue with people and interfere with their dogs, and so forth. For God's sake, let's change the subject before I lose my temper. Anyway, you're just not a hunter.

LOMOV: But you, you're a hunter? Ha! You only go hunting to get in good with the count, and to plot, and intrigue, and scheme . . . Oh, my heart! You're a schemer, that's what!

CHUBUKOV: What's that? Me a schemer? [*Shouting*] Shut up!

LOMOV: A schemer!

CHUBUKOV: You infant! You puppy!

LOMOV: You old rat! You Jesuit!

CHUBUKOV: You shut up, or I'll shoot you down like a partridge! You idiot!

LOMOV: Everyone knows that—oh, my heart—that your wife used to beat you . . . Oh, my feet . . . my head . . . I'm seeing stars . . . I'm going to faint! [*He drops into an armchair*] Quick, a doctor! [*Faints*]

CHUBUKOV: [*Going on, oblivious*] Baby! Weakling! Idiot! I'm getting sick. [*Drinks water*] Me! I'm sick!

NATALIA: What kind of a hunter are you? You can't even sit on a horse! [*To her father*] Papa, what's the matter with him? Look, papa! [*Screaming*] Ivan Vassilevitch! He's dead.

CHUBUKOV: I'm choking, I can't breathe . . . Give me air.

NATALIA: He's dead! [*Pulling* LOMOV's *sleeve*] Ivan Vassilevitch! Ivan Vassilevitch! What have you done to me? He's dead! [*She falls into an armchair. Screaming hysterically*] A doctor! A doctor! A doctor!

CHUBUKOV: Ohhhh . . . What's the matter? What happened?

NATALIA: [*Wailing*] He's dead! He's dead!

CHUBUKOV: Who's dead? [*Looks at* LOMOV] My God, he is! Quick! Water! A doctor! [*Puts glass to* LOMOV's *lips*] Here, drink this! Can't drink it—he must be dead, and so forth . . . Oh what a miserable life! Why don't I shoot myself! I should have cut my throat long ago! What am I waiting for? Give me a knife! Give me a pistol! [LOMOV *stirs*] Look, he's coming to. Here, drink some water. That's it.

LOMOV: I'm seeing stars . . . misty . . . Where am I?

CHUBUKOV: Just you hurry up and get married, and then the devil with you! She accepts. [*Puts* LOMOV's *hand in* NATALIA'S] She accepts and so forth! I give you my blessing, and so forth! Only leave me in peace!

LOMOV: [*Getting up*] Huh? What? Who?

CHUBUKOV: She accepts! Well? Kiss her, damn you!

NATALIA: He's alive! Yes, yes, I accept.

CHUBUKOV: Kiss each other!

LOMOV: Huh? Kiss? Kiss who? [*They kiss*] That's nice. I mean, excuse me, what happened? Oh, now I get it . . . my heart . . . those stars . . . I'm very happy, Natalia Stepanovna. [*Kisses her hand*] My foot's asleep.

NATALIA: I . . . I'm happy too.

CHUBUKOV: What a load off my shoulders! Whew!

NATALIA: Well, now maybe you'll admit that Squeezer is better than Guess?

LOMOV: Worse!

NATALIA: Better!

CHUBUKOV: What a way to enter matrimonial bliss! Let's have some champagne!

LOMOV: He's worse!

NATALIA: Better! Better, better, better, better!

CHUBUKOV: [*Trying to shout her down*] Champagne! Bring some champagne! Champagne! Champagne!

CURTAIN

Summer in the Country

NOT A FARCE BUT. A TRAGEDY
(1889)

ENGLISH VERSION
by ERIC BENTLEY

CHARACTERS

TOLKACHOV, *a civil servant.*
MURASHKIN, *a friend of his.*

Summer in the Country

Murashkin's apartment in St. Petersburg. The study.
Comfortable furniture. MURASHKIN *at his desk. Enter*
TOLKACHOV *holding a glass lamp globe, a toy bike, three*
hat boxes, a large parcel of clothes, a basket of beer, and
many small packages. Dazed, he looks round the room,
then sinks exhausted on the couch.

MURASHKIN: Well, how are you, my dear Ivan! Delighted
to see you. What brings you here?

TOLKARHOV: [*Breathing heavily*] My dear fellow . . . I have
a favour to ask . . . to implore of you. Lend me a revolver
till tomorrow. Be a friend.

MURASHKIN: What do you want with a revolver?

TOLKACHOV: I need one. Saints above, give me a glass of
water, will you? Water! . . . I have to have one. I've got
to get through some dark woods tonight, so just in case
. . . Be so kind. Lend me one!

MURASHKIN: Oh, you liar, Ivan Ivanovitch! What would you
be doing in dark woods? You're up to some mischief, I can
see it in your face. Now, what's the matter? Are you sick?

TOLKACHOV: Wait. Let me get my breath. Saints above, I'm
tired. I feel as if I'd been grilled on a spit. I can't stand
it any longer. Be a friend: don't ask questions, don't insist
on details, give me a revolver. I implore you!

MURASHKIN: Come, come, Ivan, what cowardice! A family
man! A Civil Servant! Shame on you!

TOLKACHOV: Family man? I'm a martyr, I'm a slave, I'm
a beast of burden. I'm a coward too—instead of marching
boldly forward into the next world, I stick around in this
one, waiting for something to turn up. I'm an imbecile.
And what's the use? Why am I alive? [*He jumps up*]

Answer me that! Why am I alive? What is behind this endless series of sufferings, mental and physical? Being a martyr to an idea, well, I could understand *that*, but being a martyr to God knows what, a martyr to a lamp shade, a martyr to a skirt! No. I beg to decline the honour. No, No, No!!!

MURASHKIN: Don't shout, Ivan, the neighbours will hear.

TOLKACHOV: Let them. What do I care! If *you* don't give me a revolver then someone else will. I'll put an end to this one way or the other, that's flat.

MURASHKIN: [*Drawing back*] Hey, careful, you've pulled that button right off. [*He refers to one of his own that* TOLKACHOV *has been inadvertently tugging at*] Calm down. I must say, I can't see what's so bad about your life.

TOLKACHOV: Bad? You can't see what's bad about it? Let me tell you then. Yes, let me tell you. It'll be a load off my mind anyway. Let's both sit down. Now just listen. Oh dear, I'm still out of breath. Phew! Well, take today, for instance. Take today. As you know, I'm in the office from ten to four. It's hot in the office, suffocating. The place is full of flies and, well, in short, my dear fellow, it's chaos. The Secretary is on leave. Krapoff is away on honeymoon. The lesser lights are crazy about summer cottages, love affairs, amateur theatricals, and you can't get any satisfaction out of them, they're always drunk or sleepy. The Secretary's work is being handled by a fellow who's both deaf in the left ear and in love. Most of our clients seem to have lost their wits. They do nothing but rush around losing their temper. Nothing but muddle and confusion. You want to scream for help. As for my work, it's absolutely deadly. The same thing over and over. An enquiry, a reference. Another enquiry, another reference. Like the waves of the sea. Your eyes are ready to drop out of your head. May I have a glass of water? You leave the office worn out, in shreds. You'd like to eat and drop into bed. But then you remember: it's summer. Vacation

time. That is to say: you're a rag, you're a piece of string.
In short, you're a slave. You have errands to do. There's
a charming custom in the country. When any of the men
goes to town, it's a matter of course for, not just his wife,
but every other country-dweller to give him lots of
errands to do. My wife sends me to the dressmaker to
scold her for making a blouse that's too wide in the bust
and too narrow in the shoulders; little Sonya's shoes must
be changed; my sister-in-law wants twenty kopecks' worth
of crimson silk to match a pattern and two and a half
yards of braid. Hold on a second, I'll read it to you. [*He
takes a note from his pocket and reads*] 'One lamp globe,
one pound ham sausage, cinnamon and cloves: five
kopecks' worth, castor oil for Misha, granulated sugar:
ten pounds. Also bring from the apartment: copper stew-
pot, sugar mortar, carbolic acid, insect powder, ten
kopecks' worth face powder, beer: twenty bottles, vinegar,
and corsets, size 82, for Miss Chanceau. And don't forget
to bring Misha's winter coat and rubbers.' Ouf! And that's
just my wife and family's list. There are also our dear
friends and neighbours, devil take them. A toy bicycle for
Volodya Vlassin, it's his birthday tomorrow. Call at the
midwife's and tell her she's needed, Colonel Vikrin's wife
is in an interesting condition. And so on. There are five
lists in my pocket. My handkerchief is all knots. My dear
Tolkachov, between leaving the office and catching the
train, you spend the time rushing round the town like a
dog with its tongue out, cursing the day you were born.
From the clothier's to the druggist's, from the druggist's
to the dressmaker's, from the dressmaker's to the pork
butcher's, from the pork butcher's back to the druggist's.
In one place, you fall and hurt yourself. In a second, you
lose your wallet. In a third, you forget to pay and they
bawl you out in front of everybody. In a fourth, you tread
on a lady's skirt. Ugh! You get so worked up and run down,
your bones ache all night, you dream of crocodiles . . .

Well, having made your purchases, how are you to carry
them. Mortar and lamp globe under one arm? The carbolic
acid with the tea? How can you manage both the beer and
the bicycle? It's a jigsaw puzzle, not to mention the labours
of Hercules! Well, you think of a few tricks, but you're
bound to spill something, and smash it goes! You take
your stand in the train with your legs apart and your arms
out like this, holding this parcel in place with your chin.
You're covered with boxes and baskets from head to foot.
The train starts up. Someone says your things are on their
seat. They push the stuff unceremoniously off onto someone else's territory. Then someone else vigorously dis-
places it yet again. A riot. Your belongings hurtle through
the air. In all directions. Someone threatens to have you
thrown out. Someone calls for the conductor. But what
can you do? [*Pause*] I just stand there blinking like a
beaten donkey. [*Pause*] Listen to this, I get to my summer
cottage. You'd think I'd be rewarded for my labours with
a drink and a good dinner, wouldn't you? And a bit of a
snooze? Not a bit of it. My wife has been in ambush quite
a time. I've hardly swallowed the soup when she sinks her
claws into me. Wouldn't I like to leave for the dance? Or
see the amateur theatricals? You can't protest. You're a
husband—the only beast of burden the S.P.C.A. won't
help out however much he's overloaded. So you see a
play called *Family Scandal* or something, clap when your
wife says so, and feel so ill you couldn't be any worse
without dropping dead. If it's a dance at the club, you
spend the time finding partners for your wife and, if
there aren't enough, you dance the quadrilles yourself.
It's after midnight when you get home. You're a wet rag,
but at last you can have your own way. Get undressed.
Go to bed. Close your eyes. Sleep. Wonderful. [*Pause*]
Pure poetry, you understand? No squealing children.
You've got rid of your wife—at last, What more could a
man want? You fall asleep. [*Pause*] What's that? Hm?

Mosquitoes. Curse them! [*He shakes his fist*] Plagues
of Egypt! Torments of the Spanish Inquisition! Mosquitoes! [*He imitates the buzzing of a mosquito*] Isn't it
plaintive, that sound? And sad? As if he wanted to beg
your pardon? But the little wretch stings so, you scratch
yourself for an hour afterwards. What to do? Smoke? Kill
mosquitoes? Cover yourself from head to foot? It's no use.
You may as well deliver yourself up to them. Let them
devour you. [*Pause*] You've no sooner accepted the mosquitoes than another torture starts. Downstairs, your wife
has guests. Singers. Tenors. A species that sleeps by day
and rehearses for amateur concerts at night. Mosquitoes
are harmless by comparison. [*He bursts into song*]

> Tell me, O tell me not
> Thy youth is quite forgot!

The pigs! To deaden the sound a bit, I've worked out this
little idea: I tap myself with my thumb—here, on the
temple—this way—till they go. They stay till four. The
moment they're gone, my wife rushes in and presents her
lawful claims to my person. Singing in the moonlight with
all those tenors, she's generated a certain amount of
ecstasy, and now she wants to work it off—on me. My dear
fellow, when she rushes into the bedroom like that, I get
so scared, I break out in a cold sweat. May I have another
glass of water? [*Pause*] Not having slept a wink all night,
you get up at six and make for the station. It's cold, and
muddy, and foggy, and you run so as not to be late, and
you get to town, and . . . well, the whole thing starts over.
There you are, my friend. A life I wouldn't wish on my
worst enemy. Horrible. I'm sick, as a result. Heartburn,
asthma, always something. Stomach trouble. My eyes cloud
over. Believe it or not: I'm mentally disturbed. [*He looks
nervously over his shoulder*] Not a word to her—but I should
like to consult a psychiatrist. There's a devil in me. When
I'm irritated, when I'm driven wild, when mosquitoes
sting, and tenors sing, everything goes black before my

eyes, and I jump up and race round the house like a lunatic shouting: 'Blood! I must have blood!' At such times I want to stick a knife into someone or smash his head in with a chair! ! [*More quietly*] That's summer in the country for you. And no one has any sympathy for me. No one sees anything wrong in all this. They even laugh. At the same time, I'm alive, you understand, so I want to live! This isn't farce, it's tragedy!! [*Pause*] If you don't want to give me a revolver, you could at least sympathize.

MURASHKIN: But I do sympathize!

TOLKACHOV: I can see how much. Well, goodbye, I still have to buy anchovies, sausages and, oh yes, tooth powder . . . before I go to the station.

MURASHKIN: Where are you living, exactly?

TOLKACHOV: Carrion Creek.

MURASHKIN: Really? Then you must know Olga Finberg, she's staying there!

TOLKACHOV: Yes, we've met, I know her personally.

MURASHKIN: That's perfectly splendid. It would be so nice of you —

TOLKACHOV: What's that?

MURASHKIN: You wouldn't mind doing me a little favour, would you? Be a friend!

TOLKACHOV: What's that?

MURASHKIN: As a friend: I implore you! First, I want you to give Olga Finberg my best. Then there's a bit of something I want you to take out to her. I got the sewing-machine she wanted, but I haven't been able to find anyone to send it by. You'll take it, won't you? Oh yes, and one other thing. That canary cage—with the canary *in* it of course! And be careful not to break the little door. Why are you looking at me like that?

TOLKACHOV: A sewing machine. A canary cage. A canary . . . Greenfinches . . . Linnets . . .

MURASHKIN: What's the matter, Ivan? You're turning purple!

TOLKACHOV: [*Stamping*] Give me that sewing machine. And where's the canary cage? [*Screaming*] Now you jump on my back! Tear me to pieces! Eat me! Make an end of me! [*He clenches his fists*] Blood! I must have blood!

MURASHKIN: You're out of your mind!

TOLKACHOV: [*Bearing down on him*] Blood! I must have blood!

MURASHKIN: [*Terror-stricken*] He's out of his mind. [*Shouts*] Petrusha! Maria! Where are you? Help!

But the servants do not appear and TOLKACHOV *continues to chase* MURASHKIN *round the room, crying: 'Blood! I must have blood!' The tension is still mounting as*

THE CURTAIN FALLS

A Wedding

A JOKE IN ONE ACT
(1889–1890)

ENGLISH VERSION
by ERIC BENTLEY

CHARACTERS

MADAM ZMEYUKIN, *a midwife.*

YAT, *a telegraph clerk.*

THE BEST MAN.

MRS. ZIGALOV, *the bride's mother.*

APLOMBOV, *the bridegroom.*

A WAITER.

DASHENKA, *the bride.*

MR. ZIGALOV, *the bride's father, civil servant, retired.*

DIMBA, *a Greek confectioner.*

A SAILOR.

NYUNIN, *an insurance man.*

'GENERAL' REVUNOV.

WEDDING GUESTS.

A Wedding

The scene is a private room in a second-rate restaurant. Brilliantly lit. Large table laid for supper. WAITERS *in tails busy at this and other tables. Behind the scenes, a band playing the last figure of a quadrille.*

Three figures cross the stage: MADAM ZMEYUKIN, *a midwife;* YAT, *a telegraph clerk; and the* BEST MAN. *The* MIDWIFE *is crying ' No, no, no!'*

TELEGRAPH CLERK: [*On her heels*] Have pity on me! [*But she keeps on crying 'No, no, no!'*]

BEST MAN: [*Following*] Now look, you can't carry on like that! Where are you going? What about the *Grand Rond? Grand Rond, s'il vous plaît!*
    [*All three are off stage*]
    [*Enter* APLOMBOV, *the bridegroom and* MRS. ZIGALOV, *the bride's mother*]

BRIDE'S MOTHER: Now, instead of bothering me with all this talk, why don't you just go and dance?

BRIDEGROOM: I can't make figure eights with my feet, I'm no Spinoza, I'm a practical man, a man of character, I find nothing amusing in idle pursuits. But dancing is not the point. Forgive me, mother dear, but there's a great deal in your conduct that I can't figure out. For example, quite apart from furniture, utensils, miscellaneous effects, you promised to give me, with your daughter, two lottery tickets. Where are they?

BRIDE'S MOTHER: My poor head, it's aching again, it must be the weather, they say it's going to thaw.

BRIDEGROOM: Don't try to wriggle out of it. You pawned those tickets. I found out only this afternoon. You're an exploiter, mother dear. Excuse the expression, but you are.

I speak without prejudice. I don't want the confounded tickets. It's a matter of principle. And I don't like being gypped. I am making your daughter the happiest of women and if you don't get those tickets back I'll make mincemeat of her into the bargain. I'm a man of honour, don't forget.

BRIDE'S MOTHER: [Counting the places at table] One, two, three, four, five . . .

A WAITER: The cook says how would you like the ice cream, ma'am?

BRIDE'S MOTHER: How do you mean: how would I like the ice cream?

WAITER: With rum, with Madeira, or with nothing, ma'am?

BRIDEGROOM: With rum, you fool. And tell the head waiter there isn't enough wine. We need some Haut Sauterne as well. [To BRIDE'S MOTHER] There was another agreement: you promised me a general. You swore to deliver a general as a wedding guest. Where is he?

BRIDE'S MOTHER: It's not my fault, my dear.

BRIDEGROOM: Whose fault is it, for heaven's sake?

BRIDE'S MOTHER: Nyunin's. The insurance man. He was here yesterday, he swore he'd dig up a general, but I suppose he just couldn't find one. We're as sorry as you are. There's nothing we wouldn't do for you. When *you* say a general, a general it should be . . .

BRIDEGROOM: Another thing. Everyone knows that telegraph clerk courted Dashenka before me. Why must you invite him to our wedding? Have you no consideration for my feelings?

BRIDE'S MOTHER: Well, er . . . what's your name again? Yes: Aplombov. My dear Aplombov, you have been married just two hours, and already you have us both worn out— me and my daughter—with your incessant talk, talk, talk. How will it be a year from now? Think of *that*.

BRIDEGROOM: So you don't like to hear the truth. I see. But that's no excuse for having no sense of honor. I want you to have a sense of honour!

[*Couples cross the stage, dancing the Grand Rond. The first couple are the* BRIDE *and the* BEST MAN. THE MID-WIFE *and the* TELEGRAPH CLERK *come last and stay behind, Enter* ZIGALOV, *the bride's father and* DIMBA, *a Greek confectioner. During the cross and afterwards in the wings, the* BEST MAN *is shouting:* 'Promenade! Promenade Messieurs-dames! Promenade!']

TELEGRAPH CLERK: [*To the* MIDWIFE] Have pity on me, enchanting one!

MIDWIFE: Listen to him . . . My dear fellow, I've told you: I am not in good voice today!

TELEGRAPH CLERK: Just a couple of notes! One! One note! Have pity on me!

MIDWIFE: You bother me. [*She sits down and vigorously uses her fan*]

TELEGRAPH CLERK: But you have no pity. A monster of cruelty, if I may so express myself, with the voice of a goddess! You've no right being a midwife with a voice like that. You should be a concert singer. Your rendering of that phrase—how does it go?—yes, um:
[*He sings*]
   I loved you though 'twas all in vain!
Exquisite!

MIDWIFE: [*Singing*]
   I loved you—and may do again!
Is that the bit you mean?

TELEGRAPH CLERK: That's it. Exquisite!

MIDWIFE: But I am not in voice today. Fan me. It's hot. [*To* BRIDEGROOM] Why are you so sad, Aplombov? On your wedding day? What are you thinking of?

BRIDEGROOM: It's a serious step—marriage. Must be given serious thought—from every angle.

MIDWIFE: What sceptics you all are! Unbelievers! I can't breathe among you. Give me air! Air! [*She practises a few notes of song*]

TELEGRAPH CLERK: Exquisite!

MIDWIFE: Fan me! My heart's about to burst! Answer me
one question: *why* am I suffocating?

TELEGRAPH CLERK: You've been sweating such a lot—

MIDWIFE: Such a word in my presence!

TELEGRAPH CLERK: Many apologies. I was forgetting you
move in aristocratic circles, if I may so express myself.

MIDWIFE: Oh, stop it. Give me poetry! Heavenly raptures!
And fan me, fan me.

BRIDE'S FATHER: [*In tipsy conversation with the* GREEK]
Another? [*Fills his glass*] Every time is the right time for a
drink. As long as your work gets done, eh, Dimba? Drink
and . . . drink and . . . drink again [*They drink*] Do you
have tigers—in Greece?

THE GREEK: [*Showing the whites of his eyes*] I'll say!

BRIDE'S FATHER: And lions?

GREEK: Lions, tigers, everything! In Russia—nothing. In
Greece—everything. That's the whole difference between
Russia and Greece.

BRIDE'S FATHER: Everything?

GREEK: Everything: my father, my uncle, all my brothers . . .

BRIDE'S FATHER: You have whales too—in Greece?

GREEK: Everything. Whales, sharks . . .

BRIDE'S MOTHER: [*To her husband*] Time to sit down, my
dear. And hands off the canned lobster—it's for the
General—I still think there'll be a General—

BRIDE'S FATHER: You have lobsters—in Greece?

GREEK: Everything! Everything I tell you—

BRIDE'S FATHER: Civil servants too?

MIDWIFE: The air must be divine—in Greece.

BRIDE'S FATHER: Have another.

BRIDE'S MOTHER: No time for another! It's past eleven.
Time to sit down!

BRIDE'S FATHER: Sit down? Good idea! Sit down! Sit down,
everyone!

　　　[*And his wife joins him in calling to all the guests, on stage
　　　and off, to take their places at table*]

MIDWIFE: [*Sitting*] Give me poetry!
His quest for storms will never cease
For only storms can bring him peace!
Give me storms!

TELEGRAPH CLERK: [*Aside*] Isn't she remarkable? I'm head over heels in love with her.

[*Enter the* BRIDE, *a* SAILOR, *the* BEST MAN, *other wedding guests. They sit down noisily. Pause. The band plays a march*]

THE SAILOR: [*Rising*] Ladies and gentlemen, as we have a great many toasts and speeches ahead of us, I propose we start at once—with the greatest toast of them all. I give you: the bride and groom!

[ALL *cry:* '*The bride and groom*' *and clink glasses and drink. The band plays a flourish*]

SAILOR: And now: it needs sweetening!

ALL: It needs sweetening.

[*The* BRIDE *and* GROOM *kiss*]

TELEGRAPH CLERK: Exquisite! Ladies and gentlemen: credit where credit is due! Let us give thanks for a splendid party in a splendid setting! What a magnificent establishment this is! Only one thing lacking: electric light—if I may so express myself. They have it all over the world. Everywhere but Mother Russia. [*He sits, sadly*]

BRIDE'S FATHER: Yes, um, electric light. Come to think of it, electric light is a hoax. They slip a piece of coal in when no one's looking. So, my good man, if you want to give us light, give us good old-fashioned light, none of these super-intellectual notions.

TELEGRAPH CLERK: Take a look at a battery some time. That's no superintellectual notion.

BRIDE'S FATHER: Certainly not! I've no wish to be caught looking at such a thing. [*Severely*] And I'm sorry to find you sympathizing with tricksters and swindlers, young man, when you should be having a drink and handing the bottle round!

BRIDEGROOM: I quite agree, father dear. Not that I object to scientific discoveries on principle. But there's a time for everything. [*To his bride*] What do you say, *ma chére?*

BRIDE: Some people like to show off and talk so no one can understand a word.

BRIDE'S MOTHER: Don't worry, my dear, your father and I never got mixed up in this education business, not in all our lives. And you're the third daughter we've found a good Russian husband for. [*To* TELEGRAPH CLERK] Why do you have to come here if you think we're so uneducated? Why not go to your educated friends?

TELEGRAPH CLERK: I respect you and your family very much, Mrs. Zigalov. I wasn't trying to show off, mentioning electric light. I've always wished Dashenka would find a good husband. And it isn't easy these days, with everyone marrying for money . . .

BRIDEGROOM: A dig at me.

TELEGRAPH CLERK: [*Scared*] That's not true! That was a . . . general observation . . . present company always excepted, if I may so express myself. Heavens, everyone knows *you're* marrying for love. The dowry isn't worth talking about.

BRIDE'S MOTHER: What? Not worth talking about, isn't it? You'd better watch your tongue. A thousand rubles in cash, three fur coats, complete furniture and liner. Try and find a dowry to match that!

TELEGRAPH CLERK: But I didn't mean . . . The furniture's splendid of course . . . I wasn't getting in any digs!

BRIDE'S MOTHER: Well, don't. We invited you on your parents' account, so don't go sticking *your* oar in. If you knew Aplombov was marrying her for money, why couldn't you have said so before? [*Tearfully*] I nursed her, I raised her, if she'd been a diamond I couldn't have treasured her more, my child, my emerald . . .

BRIDEGROOM: So you believe him! Thank you so much, thank you *so* much! [*To* TELEGRAPH CLERK] As for you,

Mr. Yat, friend of the family as you are, I cannot permit you to carry on like this in other folks' houses. Kindly take yourself off.

TELEGRAPH CLERK: How do you mean?

BRIDEGROOM: What a pity you're not a real gentleman—like myself! That being so, however, take yourself off.

[*The band plays a flourish*]

VARIOUS GENTLEMEN: [*To* BRIDEGROOM] Come off it, Aplombov, old boy! Leave him alone, old man, Don't spoil the fun. Take your seat. [*Etc.*]

TELEGRAPH CLERK: But I never . . . why, I . . . I honestly don't understand . . . Certainly, I'll go . . . But first give me the five rubles you borrowed a year ago to buy yourself a *piqué* waistcoat, if I may so express myself. Then I'll have one more drink and, um, go. But first give me the money.

THE GENTLEMEN: Take your seats. Drop it now. Much ado about nothing. [*Etc.*]

BEST MAN: [*Shouting*] To the bride's parents, Mr. and Mrs. Zigalov!

[*The cry is taken up by the others who clink and drink. The band plays a flourish*]

ZIGALOV: [*Touched, bowing in all directions*] Thank you, my friends, thank you for not forgetting us, for not snubbing us. I don't put it this way from false modesty, I have no ulterior motive, I'm not planning to cheat you in any way, I speak as I feel, in the simplicity of my heart, I begrudge you nothing, you are my friends, and I . . . I thank you!

[*He kisses those near him*]

BRIDE: [*To her mother*] Mama, you're crying! Why is that? I'm so happy!

BRIDEGROOM: Your mother's upset at the approaching separation from you. But I wouldn't advise her to forget our little talk.

TELEGRAPH CLERK: Don't cry, Mrs. Zigalov! What *are* tears, scientifically speaking? Nothing but neurotic weakness!

BRIDE'S FATHER: You have mushrooms—in Greece?

GREEK: Everything. We have everything.

BRIDE'S FATHER: Bet you don't have brown mushrooms. Like ours.

GREEK: Every kind! Every kind!

BRIDE'S FATHER: All right, Dimba, old man, now it's your turn to make a speech. Ladies and gentlemen, Mr. Dimba is going to make a speech!

ALL: A speech! Mr. Dimba! Come on, Dimba! [*Etc.*]

GREEK: But why? What for? I don't see it!

MIDWIFE: It's your turn! Make it snappy!

GREEK: [*Stands, confused*] All I can say is . . . There's Russia . . . and there's Greece . . . In Russia, there are many people . . . In Greece . . . there are many people . . . On the sea, there are ships . . . In Russia, that is . . . On land, railways . . . You are Russians, we are Greeks, I want nothing for myself. There's Russia, and there's Greece . . .

[*Enter* NYUNIN, *the aforementioned insurance man*]

INSURANCE MAN: One moment, ladies and gentlemen, just one moment! Mrs. Zigalov, may I have your attention? [*He takes her on one side*] You shall have your general. He's on his way over. A real live general aged eighty. Or maybe ninety.

BRIDE'S MOTHER: When will he get here?

INSURANCE MAN: Any minute. You'll be grateful to me till your dying day.

BRIDE'S MOTHER: A real general.

INSURANCE MAN: Well, almost real. Actually, he was in the navy. They called him Captain. That's naval lingo for General.

BRIDE'S MOTHER: You couldn't be deceiving me, could you?

INSURANCE MAN: Am I a swindler?

BRIDE'S MOTHER: Oh, no!

INSURANCE MAN: Thank you.

BRIDE'S MOTHER: It's just that I don't like to spend money for nothing.

INSURANCE MAN: Rest easy. He's a model general. [*Raising his voice for all to hear*] 'General,' I said, 'general, you've been forgetting us lately!' [*Sits down at table among the guests*] 'Pon my soul, Nyunin, my boy,' said the general to me, 'how can I go to a wedding when I don't even know the bridegroom?' 'What's wrong with the bridegroom?' I rejoined. 'Splendid, open-hearted fellow that he is!' 'What does he do?' says the general. 'Do?' says I, 'do? Why he's the valuer in a pawnshop.' 'Oh!' says the general. 'Oh what?' says I, 'the best of men work in pawnshops these days, also the best of women.' At this he clapped me on the shoulder, we smoked a Havana together, and . . .

BRIDEGROOM: When will he get here?

INSURANCE MAN: Any minute. He was putting his rubbers on when I left.

BRIDEGROOM: We must have them play a military march.

INSURANCE MAN: Bandmaster! *Marche militaire!*

A WAITER: General Revunov!

[*As the band strikes up with a march,* 'GENERAL' REVUNOV *enters.* NYUNIN *and both* ZIGALOVS *rush to greet him*]

BRIDE'S MOTHER: General Revunov, welcome to our home!

'GENERAL': Delighted I'm sure.

BRIDE'S FATHER: We aren't celebrities, General, we aren't millionaires, but don't think the worse of us on that account. We won't cheat you. We begrudge you nothing. You are welcome.

'GENERAL': Delighted I'm sure.

INSURANCE MAN: General Revunov, allow me to present the bridegroom, Mr. Aplombov, along with his newly born, I mean newly married, bride, the former Miss Zigalov. Mr. Yat of the Telegraph Office. Mr. Dimba, noted confectioner of Greek descent . . . And so forth. The rest aren't worth much. Why don't you sit down, General?

'GENERAL': Delighted I'm sure. [*But he doesn't sit down. He takes* NYUNIN *on one side*] One moment, ladies and gentlemen, a confidential conference! [*Whispering*] What do you mean: General? There are no generals in the navy! I was captain of the smallest ship in the fleet. The rank is equivalent to colonel!

INSURANCE MAN: [*Speaking over-distinctly into his ear as to a deaf man*] Let us call you General. It's simpler. These folks respect their betters. Resign yourself to being their betters!

'GENERAL': Oh. Oh, I see. [*Goes meekly back to table*] Delighted I'm sure.

BRIDE'S MOTHER: Take a seat, General. We can't give you the dainty food you're used to, but if our simple fare should take your fancy . . .

'GENERAL': [*Not following this*] What? What's that? Oh, yes. [*Long silence*] I live plainly, ma'am. Everyone lived plainly in the old days. [*Another silence*] When Nyunin invited me here, I said to him: 'That could be awkward, I don't know them.' 'What of it?' said Nyunin. 'These folk respect their betters!' 'They do?' I replied, 'well, that's different. And it's awfully boring at home.'

BRIDE'S FATHER: So you came out of pure generosity, General. How much I respect that! We're plain folks. We won't cheat you. Have something to eat, General.

BRIDEGROOM: Have you been out of the service long, General?

'GENERAL': What? Oh, yes. Very true. Yes. But what's this? This herring is bitter. This bread is bitter . . .

ALL: It needs sweetening!

    [BRIDE *and* GROOM *kiss*]

'GENERAL': [*Chuckling*] Your health, your health! [*Silence*] In the old days, everything was plain. I like that. Of course, I'm getting on. Seventy-two. Retired from the service in sixty-five. [*Silence*] On occasion, of course, they used to make a bit of a splash—in the old days . . . [*His eye lights on the sailor*] Aren't you a sailor?

SAILOR: Yes, sir.

'GENERAL': [*Relaxing considerably*] Ah! Yes. The navy. Not an easy life. Always something to think about. Every word has a special meaning. 'Top-sheets and main-sail, mast-hands aloft!' Isn't that good? And what does it mean? Your sailor knows! He, he, he!

INSURANCE MAN: To General Revunov!

[*The band plays a flourish. All cheer*]

TELEGRAPH CLERK: Thanks for telling us about the problems of the navy, General. But what about the telegraph service? You can't go in for modern telegraphy without French and German. Transmitting telegrams is no easy matter. Listen.

[*He taps out code with his fork on the table*]

'GENERAL': What does it mean?

TELEGRAPH CLERK: It means: 'Oh, how I respect all your noble qualities, General!' D'you think that's easy? Now.

[*He taps again*]

'GENERAL': Louder. I can't hear.

TELEGRAPH CLERK: [*Loudly*] 'How happy am I, dear madam, to hold you in my arms!'

'GENERAL': What madam is that? Oh. Oh yes. [*Turning to the* SAILOR] In the face of a hundred-mile-an-hour head-wind, always hoist your foretop halyards, my boy and your topsail halyards too! When the sails get loose, take hold of the foresail and foretopsail halyards and the topgallant braces...

INSURANCE MAN: Our guests are bored, Revunov, they don't understand.

'GENERAL': I'll explain. If the ship is lying with the wind on the starboard tack under full sail, and you want to bring her round before the wind, pipe all hands on deck, and as soon as they've run up, give the command: 'To your places! Round before the wind!' The men pull the stays and braces and, oh, what a life it is, in spite of yourself you leap up and shout: 'Bravo! Bravo, brave lads!'

[*He breaks off in a fit of coughing*]

BEST MAN: [*Taking advantage of this pause*] Ladies and gentlemen, we are gathered together, are we not, to do honour to our beloved . . .

'GENERAL': 'Let out the foretopsail-sheet, the topgallant-sail-sheet!'

BEST MAN: I was making a speech!

BRIDE'S MOTHER: We are only ignorant people, General. Tell us something funny!

BEST MAN: And brief.

'GENERAL': [*Not hearing*] Thank you, I've had some. Did you say beef? Er, no, thanks. The old days, yes. The life on the ocean wave. [*In a voice laden with emotion*] Tacking! Is there any joy like the joy of . . . tacking? What sailor's heart doesn't thrill to it? 'Pipe all hands on deck,' goes the cry. An electric shock runs through the crew. From captain to cabin boy . . .

MIDWIFE: I'm bored!

BEST MAN: So am I.

'GENERAL': Thank you, I've had some. Did you say pie? Er, no, thanks. [*In an exalted tone*] All eyes on the senior officer. 'Foretopsails and mainsail braces to starboard,' he cries, 'mizzen-braces to larboard, counter-braces to port!' [*He leaps up*] The ship rolls to the wind! 'Look alive, ye lubbers,' the officer cries, and fixes his eye on the topsail. Seconds of unbearable suspense. Then, it begins to flap! The ship begins to turn! 'Loose the stays, let go the braces,' yells the officer at the top of his voice. Then it's the tower of Babel. Things flying through the air, the old ship creaking in all its joints. [*Roaring*] The ship is turned! [*Silence*]

BRIDE'S MOTHER: [*Furious*] You may be a General, but you ought to be ashamed of yourself, so there!

'GENERAL': A pear? Yes, please!

BRIDE'S MOTHER: [*Louder*] You ought to be ashamed of yourself, General or no General. [*In some confusion*] Now, friends . . .

'GENERAL': [*Drawing himself up after hearing the* BRIDE'S MOTHER'S *second effort*] No general. I am no general. I am a ship's captain. Equivalent to a colonel.

BRIDE'S MOTHER: No general! And you took our money! Let me tell you, sir: we don't pay good money to get ourselves insulted!

'GENERAL': [*Bewildered*] Money? What money's that?

BRIDE'S MOTHER: You know what money. The money you took from Nyunin here. Nyunin, you made a mess of things. Engaging *this* sort of general.

INSURANCE MAN: Let's drop it. Why make a fuss?

'GENERAL': Engaged . . . money from Nyunin . . .

BRIDEGROOM: Excuse me. Didn't you accept twenty-five rubles from Mr. Nyunin here?

'GENERAL': Twenty-five rubles from Nyunin . . . [*He realizes*] Ah! So that's it. I see it all. [*Shaking his head sorrowfully*] What a dirty trick, what a dirty trick!

BRIDEGROOM: At least you got paid for it.

'GENERAL': Got paid? I did NOT get paid! [*He rises from the table*] What a trick—to insult an old man this way, a sailor, an officer who has served his country! . . . [*Muttering to himself*] If these were gentlemen, I could challenge someone to a duel, but as things are . . . [*He is distracted*] Where is the door? Waiter, show me out, waiter! [*He is leaving*] What a dirty trick! [*He has left*]

[*Pause*]

BRIDE'S MOTHER: [*To the* INSURANCE MAN] So where's that twenty-five rubles?

INSURANCE MAN: The way you carry on about trifles when people are enjoying themselves! [*Loudly*] To the happy pair! Bandmaster, a march! [*The band plays a march*] To the happy pair!

MIDWIFE: Give me air, air! I'm suffocating here!

TELEGRAPH CLERK: [*Delighted*] Exquisite creature!

[*Plenty of noise*]

BEST MAN: [*Trying to outshout the rest*] Ladies and gentlemen, we are gathered together, are we not, to do honour . . .

CURTAIN

The Celebration

A JOKE IN ONE ACT

(1891)

ENGLISH VERSION
by THEODORE HOFFMAN

CHARACTERS

KUZMA NIKOLAYEVITCH HIRIN (pronounce Héer-een). *Cashier of the Mutual Bank of N———. An irritable old man.*

ANDREY ANDREYEVITCH SHIPUCHIN (pronounce Shi-póo-cheen). *President of the Bank. In early middle age. Wears a monocle. Vain.*

TATIANA ALEXEYEVNA. *Shipuchin's wife. Age 25. Frivolous.*

NASTASIA FIODOROVNA MERCHUTKIN (pronounce Mare-chóot-keen). *A pesty old woman in an old fashioned coat.*

THREE MEMBERS OF THE BOARD OF DIRECTORS (*one of whom makes a speech*).

The Celebration

Shipuchin's office. Luxuriously furnished in a pretentious over-stuffed manner : armchairs and sofa upholstered in velvet, two desks (one very ornate), thick rugs, vases of flowers, statues, knick-knacks, and a telephone! Stage right, there is a door which leads to the lobby. In the wall, stage left, there is a small window which the president can raise to survey business or to summon his staff. Its sill is a ledge over which papers can be passed. On the sill is a bell, of the type you punch.

HIRIN *is alone, at his desk (the non-ornate one), an abacus before him, feverishly scribbling. He has wrapped a long woollen scarf several times around his neck and wears a pair of high overshoes made of heavy felt. He gets up, staggers angrily over to the window, raises it, punches the bell several times, and yells :*

HIRIN: Somebody go out and get me a fifteen kopeck box of bicarbonate of soda! And a pitcher of fresh water! How many times do I have to ask? [*Goes back to his desk, leans on it, fatigued*] I'm worn to a frazzle. I've been at this mess for three days now without shutting my eyes. Morning to night I work here, night to morning I work at home. Some life! [*Coughs*] I've got an inflammation all over me. I get hot and cold spells, my legs ache, and I keep seeing dots, dashes, and exclamation points in front of my eyes! [*Sits down*] And today that pompous windbag and swindler, our esteemed president, will deliver a report at the annual meeting: 'Our Bank: Now and in the Future.' You'd think he was the Secretary of State or something. [*Writing*] Three, oh, oh . . . two hundred, sixty eight . . . two, six, eight. He puts on his big executive

83

act, and I sit here sweating like a galley slave! He spends an hour dictating a lyrical pile of gobbledegook for an introduction, and I spend days figuring out the financial statement. Some life! I hope he goes to the devil. [*Clicks off the beads on the abacus*] I just can't take it any longer. [*Writes*] One, three, seven, oh, five . . . two, six, eight, oh . . . Oh, he's going to reward me for all this. If everything goes well and he puts it over on them again today, I get a gold medal and a three hundred ruble bonus. I'd better! [*Writes*] Because if that bonus doesn't come through, look out! I've got a temper. Get me going and there's no telling what will happen. No, sir!

> [*Offstage the sound of cheering and applause.* SHIPUCHIN's *voice is heard:* 'Thank you, my friends, thank you. I'm deeply moved.' *He enters, wearing white tie and tails. In his hands is a leather bound album which has just been presented to him*]

SHIPUCHIN: [*Addressing people outside the door*] My friends, believe me, I shall cherish this gift to my dying day as a reminder of one of the greatest moments of my life. Thanks again, and again, and again! [*He acknowledges applause with a gesture, and closes the door. Goes up to* HIRIN] And how is my old and much respected friend, Kuzma Nikolayevitch?

HIRIN: [*Getting up*] Andrey Andreyevitch, in celebrating the fifteenth anniversary of our bank, I would like the honour of congratulating you, and I sincerely hope . . .

> [*The bell has been punched as* HIRIN *starts his speech.* HIRIN *goes over and accepts a document from a hand thrust in at the window. He tries to keep talking as he submits the document to* SHIPUCHIN, *but fades out in the process*]

SHIPUCHIN: Why, thank you, old man, thanks, many thanks. You know, I think that on this glorious occasion—after all, it is a celebration—we ought to shake hands on our achievement. [*They do, solemnly and sentimentally,*

SHIPUCHIN *squeezing* HIRIN'S *shoulder with his left hand*] I want to thank you for your devotion, and thanks for everything, old man. Whatever I have managed to accomplish as president of this Bank I owe to my staff. Yes, indeed. [*Sighs*] Well, the old Bank is fifteen years old, eh? Fifteen, sure as my name's Shipuchin. [*Eagerly*] Well, how's the report coming along?

HIRIN: Good enough. Five pages to go.

SHIPUCHIN: Good! Going to be finished by three o'clock?

HIRIN: If nothing comes up to disturb me. There not too much left.

SHIPUCHIN: Excellent! Excellent! Sure as my name's Shipuchin! Let's see, the meeting's at four. Give me the first half now. I'll look it over. Here, let's have it! [*Takes it*] I'm setting great store by this report. Here we have my philosophy of finance in a nutshell. Nutshell nothing! it's a veritable skyrocket! Yes, sir, a skyrocket, that's what it is! Sure as my name's Shipuchin. [*Sits down at his desk to read the report*] Oof, I'm worn to a frazzle. Had a touch of the gout last night, and then I had to spend the whole morning racing around, what with one thing and another, and all this excitement, this ovation . . . well, it's gets you. I'm really tired.

HIRIN: [*Writing*] Two, oh, oh, three, nine . . . six, oh, five, four . . . I can't keep my eyes straight . . . Dizzy . . . three, nine, oh, six, two . . . Next . . . [*Starts flicking the abacus*]

SHIPUCHIN: Oh, there's something else that's been bothering me. Do you know, your wife stopped me again to complain about you? Said you were chasing her and your sister-in-law with a carving knife yesterday. What do you mean by that, Kuzma Nikolayevitch? Good heavens, man!

HIRIN: Andrey Andreyevitch, in honour of the celebration I'd like to ask a favour of you. [*Flaring up*] And also, considering the fact that I've been working like a slave around here, keep out of my family affairs! [*Calming down*] Please.

SHIPUCHIN: [*Sighing*] What a character you are, Kuzma Nikolayevitch. I just don't get you. Normally, you're as respectable as they come, but put a woman in front of you and you turn into Jack the Ripper. I don't see what you think is so bad about women.

HIRIN: And I don't see what you think is so good about them!

[*A pause*]

SHIPUCHIN: [*Reflecting, expansively*] The employees have just presented me with an album, and I understand that this afternoon a delegation from the Board of Directors is going to present me with a little speech and a silver tankard. [*Toying with his monocle*] Very nice, sure as my name's Shipuchin. All very just and proper. If you don't run a Bank with a little bit of style, what good is it? [*To* HIRIN] Of course, you probably know the inside story. I wrote the speech for them myself, I personally purchased the silver tankard, too. I even bought the leather folder to put the speech in. The folder alone set me back forty-five rubles, but it's worth it. Do you think that Board of Directors would have thought of such things on their own? [*Looks around him*] Take this furniture. Hand picked, and a nice little job of interior decoration it is, if I do say so myself. You know, they claim that all this is unimportant, that I'm too fastidious, being a stickler for having the brass on the doors polished, making the tellers wear decent neckties, and stationing a uniformed guard at the door. Well, my answer to that is: not one bit! That guard and that brass mean something in a bank. Now, at home I can be as vulgar as I want; eat and sleep like a pig, drink my head off . . .

HIRIN: No insinuations, if you please!

SHIPUCHIN: Insinuations? Who's making insinuations? Really you're the strangest person! I was simply saying that at home I can behave like a boor, a parvenu, do what I feel like, but here you need style. This is a Bank! It's got to impress people, it's got to have tone, dignity! [*Picks up a scrap of paper and throws it in the fire*] If I've done anything here it's to raise the reputation of this bank! Dignity, that's what counts, sure as my name's Shipuchin! [*Studies* HIRIN] Look, old man, the Board of Directors will be here any minute, and there you are sitting in those ghastly overshoes. And that scarf! And that faded old coat! You could have worn a formal outfit today at any rate; at least a dark jacket.

HIRIN: My health means more to me than any Board of Directors! I'd like you to know that I've got an inflammation all over me!

SHIPUCHIN: [*Excited*] But can't you see how sloppy you look? You're destroying the tone of the whole place!

HIRIN: If the Board of Directors comes I'll sneak out. What does it matter? [*Writes*] Seven, one, seven . . . two, one, five, oh . . . [*Flicks the abacus beads*] I don't like a mess either. Which is why you shouldn't have invited those women to the dinner tonight.

SHIPUCHIN: Stuff and nonsense!

HIRIN: Oh, I know, I know. You'll pack the hall with them, just to show off, and they'll make a mess of it for you, just watch. The only things women are good for are mischief and trouble.

SHIPUCHIN: Quite the contrary! The society of women is uplifting.

HIRIN: Hmph! All right, take your wife for instance; well-educated, highly cultured and all that, but last Monday she spilled something so confidential that it took me two days to get over it. In front of a whole bunch of people, mind you, she comes up to me and says: 'Is it true the bank's stuck with a big batch of those Dryazhko-Pryazhky stocks that have been falling? My husband's awfully worried about them!' That's the sort of thing she says in public. What gets me is why you tell women anything in the first place. They'll get you in trouble every time.

SHIPUCHIN: All right, all right! That's enough! What gloomy ideas to be throwing around a celebration! That reminds me: [*Looks at his watch*] my better-half ought to be here by now. Matter of fact I should have gone to the station to meet her, poor thing, but, well, the time's flown and anyhow I'm too tired. To be honest about it, I'm sorry she's coming. Well, I don't really mean I'm sorry. I'm glad, but it'd have been a lot better if she'd stayed at her mother's a day or two more. She'll expect me to spend the whole evening with her, and we'd sort of planned a little private party after the dinner. [*Shivers*] Oop, there it goes. I'm starting to shake already. Nerves! I'm so worn out my nerves are ready to snap on me. Get a grip on yourself. Steady, steady! There, steady as the Rock of Gibraltar, sure as my name's Shipuchin.

[TATIANA *enters, wearing a rain coat, a large travelling bag slung across her shoulder*]

Well, speak of the devil . . . Angel!

TATIANA: Darling! [*Runs to him. Prolonged kiss*]

SHIPUCHIN: We were just talking about you.

TATIANA: [*Out of breath*] Did you miss me? Are you all right? I haven't been home yet. I came straight from the station. The things I've got to tell you! No, I won't take my coat off. I just stopped in for a minute. [*To* HIRIN] How are you, Kuzma Nikolayevitch? [*To* SHIPUCHIN] Is everything all right at home?

SHIPUCHIN: Perfect. You're certainly looking fine, darling; plumper and prettier than ever. Have a good trip?

TATIANA: Wonderful! Mama and Katya send their love. Little Vassily Andreyevitch says to give you a big kiss for him. [*Kisses* SHIPUCHIN] Auntie gave me a big jar of jam for you. They're all mad at you for not writing. Zena said to give you a big kiss for her. [*Kisses him*] Oh, and if you only knew all the things that have been happening! All the things that have been happening! I'm half afraid to tell you, it's so awful. Oh, but I can

see by the look on your face that you're not happy to
see me.

SHIPUCHIN: Just the contrary, darling. [*Kisses her.* HIRIN
coughs angrily]

TATIANA: [*Sighs*] Poor Katya, poor, poor Katya. I'm so, so
sorry for her, poor thing.

SHIPUCHIN: Look, darling, we're celebrating the bank's
fifteenth anniversary today. The Board of Directors may
turn up any minute and you're not dressed properly to
receive them.

TATIANA: Of course, the celebration! 'Gentlemen, I con-
gratulate you . . . I wish you every, etcetera . . .' So today's
the celebration? And there'll be a party and a dinner. Oh,
and that wonderful speech you took so long writing for
the Board of Directors, will they deliver it to you today?
[HIRIN *coughs angrily*]

SHIPUCHIN: Darling, we don't mention such things. Now,
really, it's time you went home.

TATIANA: In a minute, in a minute. I'll tell you the whole
story in one minute and then I'll go. Right from the
beginning. Well, do you remember when you saw me off?
I sat next to that fat lady and started reading? You know
how I hate train conversations! Well, I went on reading
for three stations without saying a word to anyone. Then
evening came and I got awfully depressed. You know how
it is. There was a young man opposite me, very decent,
dark hair, not bad looking. Anyhow, we got to talking,
and a naval officer joined us, then a student or something
. . . [*Laughs*] I told them I was single—they were very
attentive after that. The one with the dark hair knew the
funniest stories and the naval officer kept singing all the
time. I laughed till my chest ached! And when the naval
officer—well, you know, navy men—when he accidentally
found out my name was Tatiana, do you know what he
sang? [*Imitating a bass voice*] 'Onyegin, I'll not deny it. I
love Tatiana madly.' [*Laughs.* HIRIN *coughs angrily*]

SHIPUCHIN: Now, Taniusha, we're interruping Kuzma Nikolayevitch's work. You run along. You can tell me all about it later.

TATIANA: Oh, I don't mind if he listens. It's all so fascinating. I'm almost finished anyway. Seriozha met me at the station and there was another young man there, some sort of tax inspector. Very handsome. He had the nicest eyes. Seriozha introduced him to me and we drove back from the station together. The weather was marvellous . . .

> [*Offstage voices :* '*You can't go in there.*' '*That's a private office!*' '*What do you want?*' '*Stop her!*' MRS. MERCHUTKIN *enters, fighting someone off. She carries a paper of some sort*]

MRS. MERCHUTKIN: Take your hands off me! What next! I want to see the manager! [*Comes over to* SHIPUCHIN] Oh, your Honour, I have the honour . . . my name is Nastasia Fyodorovna Merchutkin. My husband's in the civil service. Was.

SHIPUCHIN: What can I do for you?

MRS. MERCHUTKIN: Well, you see, your Honour, my husband was sick for five months, and while he was home, under the doctor's care, they discharged him from the civil service, for no reason whatsoever, your Honour. And when I went to collect his salary they took 24 rubles and 36 kopecks out of it, your Honour. 'What for?' I asked them. 'That's what he borrowed from the Mutual Aid Fund,' they said. What do they mean? Why should he borrow money without my consent? What sort of business is that, your Honour? I'm just a poor woman. I have to take in boarders to keep alive. I'm a poor, weak, defenceless woman, your Honour. Everybody insults me, and I don't get a kind word from anyone!

SHIPUCHIN: Excuse me. [*Takes her petition*]

TATIANA: [*To* HIRIN] But I should really tell you from the beginning. Last week I got a letter from mama. She said a certain Grendilevsky had proposed to my sister Katya. Very decent and all that, you know, but without a bit of money, not even a good job! And would you believe it? Katya actually fell for him! What a situation! Mama said I'd better get there immediately and see what I could do with Katya.

HIRIN: [*Flaring up*] I'm very sorry but you've made me lose my place. You do on gabbing about your mama and your Katya and I don't know where I am . . .

TATIANA: What of it? Really, you're the strangest creature! You should listen when a lady talks to you. And, anyway what makes you so irritable today? You're not in love, are you?

SHIPUCHIN: [*To* MERCHUTKIN] I can't make head or tail of this thing. What's the problem?

TATIANA: Of course, he's in love! Look at him blushing!

SHIPUCHIN: [*To* TATIANA] Taniusha, darling, will you please wait for me in the lobby. I'll be out in a minute.

TATIANA: Oh, very well! [*She goes out*]

SHIPUCHIN: I simply don't understand this. So far as I can tell, you've come to the wrong place, madam. This business has nothing whatever to do with us. You'll have to go to the department in the civil service where your husband was employed.

MRS. MERCHUTKIN: But, your Honour, I've been to five other places already and no one will listen to me. It was driving me crazy till my son-in-law—Boris Matveyitch, God bless his soul—gave me the idea of coming to you. 'You go to Mr. Shipuchin, mama,' he said, 'He's a big man, he's got influence. He can do anything for you.' You've got to help me, your Honour.

SHIPUCHIN: But, I can't help you, madam. Can't you understand? So far as I can make out, your husband was in the Medical Bureau of the Defence Department, and this is a purely private enterprise, a Bank! Don't you see the difference?

MRS. MERCHUTKIN: But your Honour, I've got a doctor's certificate to prove my husband was sick. There it is! Look at it! Please, look at it!

SHIPUCHIN: [*Irritated*] Yes, that's fine, fine, but I tell you it's got nothing to do with us!

[*Offstage,* TATIANA'S *laugh, followed by masculine laughter*]

SHIPUCHIN: [*Glancing towards the door*] Now she's got the clerks going! [*To* MRS. MERCHUTKIN] Look, madam, I realize it's a very complicated business. But, surely your husband must know where you should go?

MRS. MERCHUTKIN: Him? He doesn't know anything, your Honour. All he says is: 'It's none of your damned business. Get out of here!' That's all you get out of him.

SHIPUCHIN: I repeat. Your husband was in the Medical Bureau of the Defence Department, and this is a Bank, a commercial establishment, a purely private enterprise.

MRS. MERCHUTKIN: Yes, yes, I know all that, your Honour, but couldn't you at least make them pay me 15 rubles on account?

SHIPUCHIN: [*Sighing desperately*] Ohhh!

HIRIN: Andrey Andreyevitch, if this keeps up I'll never get the report finished!

SHIPUCHIN: Just one minute. [*To* MRS. MERCHUTKIN] Can't you get it through your head that it's as absurd to trouble us with this business as it would be to try get a divorce at a grocery store or the Income Tax Bureau?

[*A knock on the door*]

TATIANA: [*Outside*] Andrey, can I come in?

SHIPUCHIN: [*Shouting*] Wait a minute, darling, wait a minute! [*To* MRS. MERCHUTKIN] Maybe they are cheating you, but what's that got to do with us? We're having a celebration today, it's our fifteenth year in business. Someone might come in any minute. Please, let me alone!

MRS. MERCHUTKIN: Your Honour, have pity on a poor orphan! I'm a weak, defenceless woman. I'm worn out

and worried to death. My boarders are suing me, I've got
this business on my hands, I have to run the house, and
my son-in-law's out of a job!

SHIPUCHIN: My dear lady, I . . . I . . . No! Look, I can't
talk to you! My head's spinning. You're wasting our time,
and your own, too. [*Sighs, aside*] She's an idiot, sure as
my name's Shipuchin! [*To* HIRIN] Kuzma Nikolayevitch,
please explain to the lady, that . . . [*Goes out of the office
with a vague wave of his hand*]

HIRIN: [*Going up to her, angry*] Well, what do you want?

MRS. MERCHUTKIN: I'm a weak defenceless woman. I may
look strong, but if you gave me an operation you'd see
that not one part of my body's normal. I can hardly stand
on my feet, and I didn't even enjoy my coffee this morning.

HIRIN: All I asked was a simple question. What do you want?

MRS. MERCHUTKIN: Just tell them to pay me fifteen rubles
now. The end of the month is all right for the rest.

HIRIN: But you've just been told in plain words: This is a
Bank!

MRS. MERCHUTKIN: I know, I know, and if you want I can
show you the medical certificate.

HIRIN: Is that a head on your shoulders, or what is it?

MRS. MERCHUTKIN: My dear sir, all I'm asking is: do I get
what's coming to me or not? I'm not interested in anybody
else's money, just mine.

HIRIN: And all I'm asking, my dear madam, is: have you
got a head on your shoulders or not? And I'm damned if
I'm going to waste my time talking to you. [*Pointing to
the door*] Will you kindly leave!

MRS. MERCHUTKIN: [*Surprised*] But what about the money?

HIRIN: That's not a head, it's a block of . . . [*Taps on the
desk to indicate wood, and then taps his forehead. Repeats
the two gestures for her benefit*]

MRS. MERCHUTKIN: [*Offended*] Oh, it is, is it? Well, you
listen to me! You can talk to your own wife that way, but
my husband's in the civil service. You just watch your step!

HIRIN: [*Losing his temper, choking*] Get out!

MRS. MERCHUTKIN: Just try and make me!

HIRIN: [*Barely controlling himself*] If you don't get out of here this minute, I'll call the guard and have you thrown out! Now, get out! [*Stamping his foot*]

MRS. MERCHUTKIN: Don't think you can scare me! I've met your type before, you skinflint!

HIRIN: Never in my life have I seen a harpy like this! Ooh, my head's swimming! [*Breathing hard*] I'm telling you for the last time. Do you hear me? If you don't get out of this room, you old bat, I'll grind you to smithereens! I'm warning you! I've got a temper! I might cripple you for life! I might commit a crime!

MRS. MERCHUTKIN: Ah, your bark is worse than your bite! You can't scare me! I know your type.

HIRIN: [*In despair*] I can't stand the sight of her. I'm sick. I can't take it any longer! [*Goes to his desk and sits down*] The place is infested with females! I'll never get finished, never!

MRS. MERCHUTKIN: Am I asking for other people's money? No! All I want is what's coming to me, my legal rights. [*Noticing* HIRIN'S *overshoes*] Why, you ought to be ashamed of yourself! Sitting in a fancy office in your galoshes! You lowbrow!

[SHIPUCHIN *and* TATIANA *enter*]

TATIANA: Then the Berezhnitskys gave a party. Katya wore a pale blue foulard silk dress, very low cut in front. It went beautifully with her hair, all piled up on top of her head. I set it for her myself. When that girl is properly dressed, with her hair done right, she's simply fascinating.

SHIPUCHIN: [*Suffering from a migraine attack*] Yes, yes, fascinating . . . fascinating . . . They might get here any minute.

MRS. MERCHUTKIN: Your Honour!

SHIPUCHIN: [*Despondently*] You still here? What can I do for you?

MRS. MERCHUTKIN: Your Honour, this man here [*Pointing at* HIRIN]—yes, him, that's the one—he tapped on the desk and then he tapped his head, that's what he did! You told him to take care of my case, and all he's done is be sarcastic and insult me. I'm a weak, defenceless woman, your Honour . . .

SHIPUCHIN: Very good, madam, I will look into the matter at the first opportunity. Only go away. Come back later. [*Aside*] I can feel the gout coming on.

HIRIN: [*Goes quietly up to* SHIPUCHIN] Andrey Andreyitch, send for the guard. Have him throw her out on her ear. How long can we take it?

SHIPUCHIN: [*Alarmed*] Good God, no, no! She'll start screaming and everyone in the building will know about it.

MRS. MERCHUTKIN: Your Honour . . .

HIRIN: [*In a tearful voice*] But I have to finish the report. I won't get it done on time! [*Goes back to his desk*] I give up.

MRS. MERCHUTKIN: Your Honour, when do I get the money? I need it right away.

SHIPUCHIN: [*Aside, with indignation*] The most horrible, repulsive hag I've ever . . . [*To* MRS. MERCHUTKIN, *softly*] I have already informed you, madam, that this is a Bank, a private enterprise.

MRS. MERCHUTKIN: Don't be cruel, your Honour. Be a father to me. If the medical certificate isn't enough I'll get an affidavit from the police. Tell them to give me the money!

SHIPUCHIN: [*Worn out*] Ooof!

TATIANA: But, my dear woman, really, you're the strangest person. They've already told you that you're only in the way. You shouldn't go round bothering people.

MRS. MERCHUTKIN: Lady, you tell them. No one will help me. Not even eating and drinking mean anything to me any more. I didn't even enjoy my coffee this morning.

SHIPUCHIN: [*Exhausted*] All right! How much do you want?

MRS. MERCHUTKIN: Twenty-four rubles and thirty-six kopecks.

SHIPUCHIN: Very well. [*Takes the money out of his wallet*] There's twenty-five rubles. Keep the change, and get out of here!

[HIRIN *coughs angrily*]

MRS. MERCHUTKIN: [*Hiding the money*] Oh, thank you kindly, your Honour. Thank you. [*She starts out, but stops at the door*]

TATIANA: [*Sitting on* SHIPUCHIN'S *desk*] I really ought to be going. [*Looks at her watch*] Oh, but I didn't finish telling you. It'll just take a minute, then I'll go. It was horrible! At the Berezhnitskys! Oh, the party was all right, so-so, but nothing special. Naturally, Katya's admirer, Grendilevsky, was there, but I'd had a talk with Katya. I cried a little, and told her off, and she agreed to have it out with Grendilevsky at the party. So, she told him 'No,' and I thought: Well, that's that, Mama's happy, Katya's saved, maybe I can begin to have a little fun. But what do you think happened? Katya and I were walking in the garden when suddenly . . . All of a sudden we heard a—shot! [*Excited*] Just the thought of it upsets me. [*Fans herself with her handkerchief*] It's all I can do to tell you about it.

SHIPUCHIN: [*Sighs*] Ohhh . . .

TATIANA: [*Weeping*] We ran to the summer house, and there . . . there was poor Grendilevsky . . . stretched out on the ground . . . with a pistol in his hand!

SHIPUCHIN: I can't stand it! I can't stand it another minute! [*Sees* MRS. MERCHUTKIN] What do you want *now?*

MRS. MERCHUTKIN: What about my husband's job, your Honour? Can he have it back?

TATIANA: [*Weeping*] He'd aimed straight at his heart. Here! Katya fainted dead away, the poor creature! And he almost died of fright. He just lay there, white as a sheet, and asked us to get a doctor. Then the doctor came . . . and saved the poor creature's life . . .

MRS. MERCHUTKIN: Can't my husband have his job back, your Honour?

SHIPUCHIN: No! I can't stand it, I can't stand it! [*Breaks down, weeping*] I just can't take it any longer. [*Holds out both hands to* HIRIN, *imploringly*] Get rid of her! Get her out of here! Help me!

HIRIN: [*Goes to* TATIANA] Get out of here!

SHIPUCHIN: Not her! The other one! That monster, there! [*Pointing to* MRS. MERCHUTKIN]

HIRIN: [*Not understanding. To* TATIANA] Get out! Get out! Get out! [*Stamping. Advancing*]

TATIANA: What? What do you mean? Really, you're the strangest person! Have you gone mad?

SHIPUCHIN: [*Oblivious*] This is awful! I'll have a breakdown! Get rid of her! Kick her out!

HIRIN: Get out of here! I'll break every bone in your body! I'll cripple you for life! I'll commit a crime!

[TATIANA *runs away from him. He chases her*]

TATIANA: How dare you, you crazy fool! [*Shouts*] Andrey! Help! Andrey! [*Screams*]

SHIPUCHIN: [*Chasing after them*] Stop it! Stop it! Let her alone! For God's sake, shut up! Stop yelling! Think of our reputation!

HIRIN: [*Starts chasing* MRS. MERCHUTKIN] Get out! Get out! Catch her! Beat her up! Cut her throat!

SHIPUCHIN: [*Shouting*] Stop shouting! Please, please, for God's sake, cut it out!

MRS. MERCHUTKIN: Holy saints in heaven! Holy saints! [*Squealing*] Holy saints alive!

TATIANA: [*Screaming*] Help, help! Save me! I'm going to faint! I'm going to faint!

[*Jumps on a chair, then falls on a sofa, moaning*]

HIRIN: [*Chasing* MRS. MERCHUTKIN] Let me at her. Kill her! Kill her! Smash her to pieces! Chop her to bits!

[*A loud knocking at the door. A voice:* 'A delegation from the Board of Directors']

SHIPUCHIN: Delegation . . . reputation . . . situation . . .

HIRIN: Get out! All of you, you damned females! [*Rolling up his sleeves*] Let me at 'em! I'm going to commit a crime!

> [*The delegation enters, three formally dressed gentlemen. One holds the leather bound 'little speech,' another a silver tankard.* TATIANA *is still moaning, her face buried in the couch.* MRS. MERCHUTKIN *has leaped into* SHIPUCHIN'S *arms, also moaning. He drops her and sinks into his desk chair.* HIRIN *freezes, and then tries to efface himself: rolls down his sleeves, smiles*]

ONE OF THE DIRECTORS: [*Reads aloud*] To the honourable and most respected Andrey Andreyevitch Shipuchin: To cast a retrospective glance at the history of this financial institution of ours, and review its steady expansion in the mind's eye, is to glow with extreme satisfaction. In its early struggle for existence, lack of capital, and failure to develop a satisfactory volume of business compelled us to heed Hamlet's profound question: 'To be or not to be?' Voices of defeatism proposed surrender and dissolution. Then you assumed the presidency. Your wide knowledge, your boundless energy, and your consummate tact have resulted in extraordinary success, in uninterrupted expansion. The dignity and reputation of the bank . . . [*coughs*] . . . reputation of the bank . . .

MRS. MERCHUTKIN: [*Moaning*] Ohh, ohhh . . .

TATIANA: [*Moaning*] Water! Water!

THE DIRECTOR: [*Continuing*] . . . reputation of the bank has been elevated to such a pinnacle that our financial institution can now regard itself as the equal of any bank here or abroad . . .

SHIPUCHIN: [*Completely gone*] Reputation . . . delegation . . . situation . . . 'Tell me not in mournful numbers life is but an empty dream . . .'

DIRECTOR: [*Continuing in confusion*] Then, as we proudly survey the present situation with an objective eye, we feel,

most honourable and highly respected Andrey Andreyevitch, that . . . [*To the others*] Perhaps we'd better come
back later . . . Yes, later, much later . . .

They leave in confusion. HIRIN *bows, closes the door, and
resumes his pursuit of the women, who scream, at the*

CURTAIN

THE SQUARE ROOT OF LOVE

(ALL GROUPS—FOUR COMEDIES)

By DANIEL MELTZER

1 man, 1 woman—4 Simple Interiors

This full-length evening portrays four preludes to love—from youth to old age, from inno-
cence to maturity. Best when played by a single actor and actress. **The Square Root of
Love.** Two genius-level college students discover that Man (or Woman) does not live by
intellectual pursuits alone . . . **A Good Time for a Change.** Our couple are now a suc-
cessful executive and her handsome young male secretary. He has decided it's time for a
change, and so has she . . . **The Battling Brinkmires.** George and Marsha Brinkmire, a
middle-aged couple, have come to Haiti to get a "quickie" divorce. This one has a surprise
ending . . . **Waiting For To Go.** We are on a jet waiting to take off for Florida. He's a retired plumbing contractor who thinks his life is over—she's a recent widow returning to
her home in Hallandale. The play, and the evening, ends with a beginning . . . A success
at off-off Broadway's Hunter Playwrights. Requires only minimal settings.   (#21314)

SNOW LEOPARDS

(LITTLE THEATRE—COMIC DRAMA)

By MARTIN JONES

2 women—Exterior

This haunting little gem of a play was a recent crowd-pleaser Off Off Broadway in New
York City, produced by the fine StageArts Theatre Co. Set in Lincoln Park Zoo in Chicago
in front of the snow leopards' pen, the play tells the story of two sisters from rural West
Virginia. When we first meet Sally, she has run away from home to find her big sister Claire
June, whose life Up North she has imagined to be filled with all the promise and hopes so
lacking Down Home. Turns out, life in the Big City ain't all Sally and C.J. thought it would
be: but Sally is going to stay anyway, and try to make her way. "Affecting and carefully
crafted . . . a moving piece of work."—New York City Tribune. *Actresses take note*: this
play is a treasure trove of scene and monologue material. *Producers take note*: the play
may be staged simply and inexpensively.   (#21245)